Exam Magic®

How to

survive school

(handwritten: "enjoy" with arrow pointing to "survive")

MICHAEL WARWICK

FLORENCE MAY
Publishing

London
www.florencemaypublishing.com
www.exammagic.co.uk

First published in the UK by Florence May Publishing in 2016

42 Sherringham Avenue Tottenham, London N17 9RN

Copies are available at discount rates for bulk orders. Contact sales
on 0208 720 7126 or email sales@florencemaypublishing.com

ISBN 978-0-9956532-0-7

British library Cataloguing in Publication Data

A catalogue record for this book is available from the British
Library.

Edited by: Catherine E Oliver - www.oliver-editorial.com
Illustrated by the author
Cover design: Florence May Publishing

Printed in the UK by Lightning Source Ltd

To Nana
My guiding star.
&
To the communities of students, parents and teachers
who make this work possible.

*"Everyone has been made for some particular work, and the desire
for that work has been put into every heart."*

—Rumi

ACKNOWLEDGEMENTS

Thanks to all of the people who encouraged the making of this book. There are too many to mention by name, but some must be given special thanks: Danielle K Watts for life-changing advice and guidance. Ayse Enver Yusuf for championing Exam Magic and asking for more and better resources for her students. Jim and Sharon Adams for their enthusiasm and support. Scott Cohen and Liviu Babitz for their friendship and expertise. Vikki and Toby Skinner for going over the manuscript with a fine-tooth comb. Seth Godin for responding to my emails. Nick Troop for coffee, cakes and data crunching. Sherife Tayfun for walking the talk and lighting the way. Louise Barnard for her brilliant ideas. My parents for believing in me. And of course Chiara D'Anna for her love and patience.

Most of all I want to thank all of my students for challenging and motivating me to bring my best self to school.

Michael Warwick

TABLE OF CONTENTS

INTRODUCTION

Do you have exams to take?

If you're worried that you might not get the exam results you want, you're not alone. This book came about because a teacher wanted to help his students stop worrying and get the best exam results possible.

Let's start with an obvious fact; at least, it's obvious once you see it. Do you realise that exams are not passed in the exam hall?

Exams are passed in your bedroom, or at the kitchen table or in the library or online, and in your classroom with your teachers. Wherever you do the preparation and study is where the exam is passed. The better the preparation, the better the exam results.

Imagine that you are a musician or an actor and you have to perform a new song or play in front of an audience. Would you practice before you went on stage? Of course you would.

The problem with practicing or studying for exams is that we've all got plenty of other things we'd rather be doing. Plus there's the fear. We have fears and doubts about how our exam results could affect our future and about our ability to pass the exams. On top of it all, it's not nice feeling judged.

Let's put it another way: Do you accept that preparing for exams is the best way to pass them? If so, then we need to be honest about what gets in the way of doing that effectively, and then we need to use strategies to overcome those obstacles. That's what this book is for.

WHY I WROTE THIS BOOK

Here's how this book came into being: I was running an Exam Magic programme in a school and everything was going very well. The school liked the work so much that they asked me if I would take the whole of the upper school off timetable for the afternoon and 'do something with them'. I should've said no. The interventions I deliver have been developed and tested over many years so that they work. To attempt an untested workshop with so many students, for a whole afternoon, was foolhardy, but I was eager to please, so I agreed, coming up with the idea of the group's writing a book together. The students would identify all of the problems that they are grappling with and then work in teams to come up with strategies and solutions to solve them.

What I hadn't realised was that almost a third of the students in the room were feeling very vulnerable and in some cases overwhelmed by the pressures of school. Many students were not, at that moment, able to access the resilience needed to go through the process I was facilitating, and I hadn't thought the idea through sufficiently to support them with it.

A significant number of students disengaged from the work, and as the room lost momentum, I began to wobble.

A lot of teachers go through this kind of thing. You start to sweat, and sometimes you hear your own voice as if it's coming from outside of yourself. It can feel like rolling a boulder uphill when the group energy splits like this. I actually got so flustered that I mistimed the workshop and finished ten minutes early, by which point I'd lost the whole group, and because we were using lots of paper and pens, the hall was a mess.

To make it even more fun for my ego, there were staff from the school in attendance who seemed to me to be watching in horror, but not really helping out. I was, after all, meant to be the big-shot expert from London!

In the end, I felt like the session went so badly, I just wanted to put the whole thing behind me and forget about it. I took all of the work the engaged students had made and stored it in my basement at home. The fact that I had publicly announced the intention to write a book slipped my mind.

Some months later, I attended a large motivational event with a very well-known British speaker. He announced from the stage that if anyone would read three books, he would personally mentor them free of charge. I took him at his word and read all three books. I got a lot out of the experience, and I'm thankful to him for that, but when I contacted his secretary to arrange the mentoring, I was met with a bemused comment about the speaker 'often getting carried away' and 'saying all kinds of things from the stage'.

At first I was angry and felt cheated. How could anyone be so irresponsible? Then I realised that I had done a very similar thing. What a valuable lesson. I vowed then and there always to keep my word, and so down I went into the basement and up came the students' worksheets. I began to piece this book together from their insights, adding ideas of my own from my experience of over a decade running workshops to help young people make the most of their education.

If anything, this book is a testament to resilience. It demonstrates that no matter how difficult things get, we can all dig deep and find the energy and willingness to do the best thing for ourselves and for those we love and care for.

I'm probably over that experimental workshop now, because I can write about the experience without breaking into a sweat, and I'm sharing the story with you so you won't feel so bad when things seem to be going wrong for you, too.

It's impossible to do anything worthwhile without putting in sustained effort, and things won't always go the way you want them to. Learning to pick yourself up, dust yourself off and find new ways around the problems and challenges in front of you is what this book is all about.

How to Use This Book

Here are a couple of quick tips on how to get the most out of this book.

1. Use the Problems and Strategies list

This book describes thirty problems identified by a group of students, just before they took their GCSEs in year 11. If you're outside of the UK, GCSEs are the exams you take around the age of 16. In the USA, for example, they would be similar to the exams you take to graduate from high school.

For each problem, students provided a suggestion on how to get past it. Exam Magic expanded on the suggestions, so you'll find advice on how to solve your problems and pass your exams with maybe even better results than you think you can get right now. Exam Magic is the name of a method I developed to help students, parents and teachers find effective solutions to the challenges that exams present. I chose the name because I hoped it would catch people's imaginations, but it's not really about magic. The Exam Magic method is a fun and easy way to understand the science behind what works best when it comes to learning and passing exams. It's science that works like magic, because it helps you to access the incredible power of two of your most magical of possessions—your brain and your mind!

You can scan the Problems and Strategies list and see which problems you relate to most. If you want to read the whole book from cover to cover, then feel free to do that if you're interested, but you probably won't need to unless you can relate to every single problem.

2. Start conversations
A second and very important way to use this book is to help your teachers and parents understand what you're struggling with or worried about.

Have you ever felt misunderstood by the adults in your life, whether family members or teachers? That was a rhetorical question, by the way. Of course you've been misunderstood; it's hard to communicate clearly sometimes and especially when we're under a lot of pressure. That's why the book will sometimes suggest that you underline or highlight the parts that apply to you and show them to a teacher or parent. The book can help adults see the problem from your point of view, so you can use the book as a way of starting conversations about the help you might need to meet the challenges in front of you.

Two Key Ideas at the Heart of This Book

Before we get into the discussions of specific problems and strategies, we need to talk about two important ideas that you'll need to understand to get the most out of this book. One involves the way you think about school, and the other involves the way you think about stress and fear.

Think about school in a different way
A central Exam Magic idea is that to do your best work, with the least amount of stress, you need to think about school in a different way.

This might not apply to you, but as a teacher I think that sometimes students feel like education is something that's being done to them or that they're working to please other people—mainly their parents and teachers.

If you think about it, most people don't get to choose whether they go to school or not. Often you don't get to choose which school you go to or who your teachers are. You do get to choose some of your subjects, but not all of them. You get put into groups, and teachers make and enforce the rules, and if the school has a uniform policy, they even tell you what clothes you can and can't wear. Does this all sound familiar?

So overall, it can sometimes feel as if education is being forced on you, rather than being something you're benefitting from.

But imagine this: What if all of the teachers came to school and set up their classrooms, the site staff and cleaners made the place safe, clean and tidy, and the catering staff cooked the meals, but no students turned up? How long would a school stay open without its students?

What if the opposite happened? What if all of the students turned up, but the building had no heating or lighting and no school meals? What if the students were wandering from classroom to classroom and there were no teachers to speak to or lessons to go to? How long would that continue?

School exists for you, and the teachers are there for you. Without you, there would be no school. Conversely, if there were no teachers, there'd be no-one to help you learn, and you'd be wasting your time going there.

Your school is there to help you get the education you need to move on to the next stage of your life. Everything's been set up for you. The teachers have trained to be able to help you, the building has been built, and the computer suites, the labs and the sports facilities have been put together—all to help you get what you need out of the experience.

Maybe that's not the way it feels some of the time, but can you see the logic in it? Your education is for your benefit and requires your participation.

How many times have you been in class, not understanding the teacher's instructions but keeping your hand down for fear of embarrassing yourself? Getting the best out of school involves doing the work and asking for help when you need it.

Think about fear in a different way

Speaking of embarrassment, I'd like to cover one more big idea before you move on to the Problem and Strategy pages. It has to do with a massive secret that few people seem happy to talk about. It has to do with stress.

Stress is a code word for fear

Adults generally don't like admitting that they're afraid, so they made up the word 'stress' to use instead.

So when I say I'm stressed, what I really mean is that I'm afraid of making a mistake, or being laughed at, or getting left behind or left out or of not being able to do something and looking silly.

I could be afraid that I'll not cope with all the things I have to do and I'll be shamed for it. I could be afraid that people don't or won't like me or that I'll never get a job or get into college or university. I could be afraid of letting my parents down, or afraid that I'm not attractive enough and I'll never get a boyfriend or girlfriend.

The list of things that scare us can be pretty long, but we can learn to change our relationship to fear by understanding it better. To understand it better we'll need a few concepts to help us.

Meet the Fear Monkey

One of the concepts you'll be reading about in this book involves the Fear Monkey. The Fear Monkey is a way to talk about fear—where it comes from and how it affects the way we feel. We don't have a real Fear Monkey, of course, but the metaphor has been used for thousands of years to explain how our minds and bodies work.

Look at Diagram 1 on page 17; it shows what's called a Monkey Mind Map. You'll see that the Fear Monkey is guarding a line it doesn't want you to cross. That line is called the *fear barrier,* and it's the outermost limit of your familiar zone.

Your *familiar zone* contains everything you've got used to up until now. The stuff in your familiar zone is represented on the diagram by the dots in circles. This zone contains your home, the people you know, the places you go, the things you do, the thoughts and beliefs you have about yourself, the thoughts you think about other people, and what you think other people think about you.

Your familiar zone does not contain your hopes and dreams. They live outside your familiar zone and are represented by the dots that look a little bit like stars on the other side of the fear barrier. To make your hopes and dreams reality, you have to be willing to cross your fear barrier.

Every time you cross the fear barrier, your familiar zone gets a little bit bigger. If you cross the fear barrier over and over again, your familiar zone keeps growing until it includes your hopes and dreams and you get to live them for real. If you refuse to cross the fear barrier, your life actually begins to shrink. Ever felt trapped? That's the fear barrier closing in on you.

We all have to keep facing our fears if we want to keep expanding our lives. It's almost as if we're playing a game and those are the rules. Knowing the rules gives us a better chance of winning than does just running around hoping for the best. That makes sense, doesn't it?

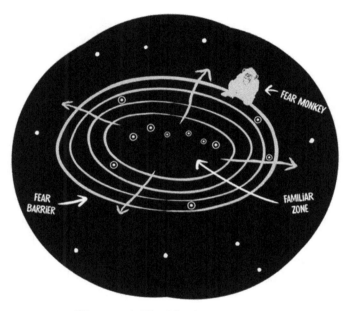

Diagram 1: The Monkey Mind Map

Your Fear Monkey loves you

So, why does the Fear Monkey want to stop us from crossing the fear barrier?

Simply put, it believes it's keeping us safe. Our Fear Monkeys love us and want us to stay alive. It's a metaphor for an older part of our psychology that deals with survival. There was a time when leaving the people and places we knew and going into unfamiliar territory was dangerous, and the Fear Monkey remembers this.

Diagram 2: The original purpose of the Fear Monkey

So the Fear Monkey is here to help us survive, but it often gets things wrong and tries to protect us from new things that aren't actually a threat to our survival and that could even be useful to us—things like asking for help with exams, for example. Broadly speaking, the Fear Monkey is uncomfortable with unfamiliar situations and really hates the idea of being left out, being embarrassed or getting things wrong.

Things the Fear Monkey says

Maybe you recognise some of the things the Fear Monkey says when it's frightened. It says...

- **I'm afraid...** I'm afraid this might go wrong, I'm afraid they might not like me, I'm afraid I'll get lost, I'm afraid I'll be embarrassed, I'm afraid I can't do it, I'm afraid, ... You fill in the blank.

- **I don't know…** I don't know if this will work out, I don't know what to do, where to go, what to say, etc.
- **This is hard, so best leave it until…** Best leave it 'till I feel ready, I'm stronger, I'm older, I've had more practice and so on and so on.

Are you familiar with these Fear Monkey sayings?

Fear Monkey thoughts cause fearful feelings and corresponding physical sensations. You might feel your throat tighten, or your breathing could get shallow or your heart might race. Your muscles might get tense, your thoughts might spin and you could feel sick in the stomach.

It takes courage to step forward into these uncomfortable feelings, but that's exactly what you do each time you cross the fear barrier and expand your familiar zone.

What will the others think of me?
Another thing the Fear Monkey worries about is, 'What will the others think of me?'

There was a time when we needed our tribe to care for us and protect us from wild animals and other threats. If we got rejected by our own people, then our lives would be at risk. Going into new or unfamiliar territory could end up with us being eaten by a lion, for example. Most of the time it's not like that anymore, but the Fear Monkey hasn't figured that out yet.

Whenever we turn back into our familiar zones and retreat from our fear barriers, our Fear Monkeys relax and we feel better.

So is the answer not to try to cross the fear barrier at all? Clearly not!

Dealing with your Fear Monkey

Giving in to the Fear Monkey isn't the way to go, at least not if you want your life to be full of the things, places, people, experiences and exam results that you really want. The new things and experiences we want can't be dragged into our familiar zones, so we have to expand those zones to grow our lives.

If we let our Fear Monkeys keep us stuck, we stay with things as they are now. New stuff happens, but it's not the stuff we choose, because we're not taking action.

Does this make sense to you?

We've got to learn to take action even when we're not sure it'll work out and when we're afraid of embarrassment and it seems difficult. Success in exams happens when you spend more of your time dealing as best you can with the Fear Monkey and expanding your familiar zone by taking action. That's what this book will help you do.

It sounds like work!

It does take work to get good at anything worthwhile, whether it's exams or sports or art or science or music or cooking or whatever! It all takes practice to improve. Have you ever noticed how difficult it can be to get started with something you don't know how to do? Sometimes it feels totally overwhelming and we don't even know where to begin.

This is where we really have to watch out for the Fear Monkey.

One of its favourite lies is: 'You've got to solve all of your problems all at once; if you don't know how, if you can't solve it now, then you should just give up—it's impossible!'

But that's not true. The Fear Monkey loves to exaggerate. It has an all-or-nothing type of personality. Either you are brilliant or you are a failure. Either you can do it perfectly or you should give up.

None of what the Fear Monkey says is true. It *feels* true because of the fear we feel when we listen to its monkey mind chatter, but it's not true.

The truth is that we work things out, bit by bit, as we go along. All that's needed is the courage and determination to take little steps past the Fear Monkey's thinking, move through the fear barrier and keep on growing as human beings. That's what you're in school to do. You're in school to grow into being more of yourself.

I'm not saying you won't get judged. This isn't going to be a piece of cake, and you'll probably get knock-backs, but then who said life was meant to be easy?

We need challenges to keep us interested. What we don't need is to allow ourselves to be controlled by our Fear Monkeys.

Over to you
Now that you know about thinking about school in a different way, along with the Fear Monkey and the familiar zone, it's time to dive into the Problems and Strategies pages.

There's also a website, **www.exammagic.co.uk**, where you can get more help and advice and watch videos of students talking about their exam experiences. You can join the site for free and download a relaxation Audio Patch that helps you calm your Fear Monkey and focus your mind on finding solutions to the challenges you're facing. You'll also find the relaxation Audio Patch as The Exam Magic App for Android on **Google Play** and for Apple on the **App Store**.

Finally, let me say just this one thing. Life is full of challenges, and how we meet those challenges decides the quality of the lives we lead. If we run and hide, our lives tend to stay too small for comfort. If we're brave enough to face the Fear Monkey, our lives keep on expanding and getting better.

Exams are a big challenge, and Exam Magic is here to help you face it.

Wishing you lots of happiness.

Very Best,
Michael Warwick
Exam Magic 2016

PROBLEMS AND STRATEGIES

PROBLEM #1: THERE'S TOO MUCH PRESSURE ON ME

Here's what students said about this problem:
'Don't try to do too much at once.'

Exam Magic says:
While you're working towards your exams, you'll probably have the feeling that you're not 'doing it right'. Everyone who is working to expand their familiar zone feels like they aren't doing it right. That's normal.

Remember that the Fear Monkey—the primitive part of ourselves that responds to threats—deals in 'either-or' thinking. When we're listening to the Fear Monkey, it will tell us that either we have to get something perfect or it's not good enough. That's just one of its tricks. It also tells us either that we're able to solve everything all at once or that it's hopeless and we should give up.

Don't believe it.

Chunk your studying down and expand your familiar zone moment by moment. Keep going, doing a little bit at a time.

You're not imagining it
There *is* too much pressure on you.

Many adults think our educational system shouldn't put so much pressure on you. Especially as it gets close to exam time, the amount of work that needs doing can be huge.

What *isn't* true is that you won't be able to cope with it. You don't have to like it, and it's probably not fair that you have to cope with it, but you *can* cope, even if it feels like sometimes you can't.

If you are reading this and there's a voice inside that agrees with the sentence above, then that's your inner courage speaking. One good thing about pressured situations is that the brave voice gets forced to show itself. It's good to know it's there, even if we often forget about it.

On the other hand, there are times when our inner courage just can't get through and we don't hear it. If you should ever find yourself in a situation like that, speak to someone about it. Sometimes we need specialist help with pressure and stress.

If you're too shy or not sure how to start a conversation about it, show an adult this section and that will help them begin to understand what the situation is. Sometimes we feel better after we've got something that's worrying us off our chests.

We all let our problems get the better of us at one time or another. Try to keep in mind that problems can often be solved, and if they can't be solved, at least they can be understood.

PROBLEM #2: MY PARENTS NAG ME AND DON'T UNDERSTAND THE PRESSURE I'M UNDER

Here's what students said about this problem:
'Ask your parents to test you.'

Exam Magic says:
This could work. At least your parents will see that you're studying. They might still nag you, but if you involve them, they'll have a reason to ease off a little. Is this something you can see yourself doing? Invite your parents to read this book; they might give the testing a go. My experience with parents is that they *want* to help but don't always know how to.

Many teachers agree that there's a lot more pressure on students today than any of us remember from the past. Depending on how old your parents are, they might not be aware of the pressure you're feeling because school felt different for them.

If your parents can't be expected to know what it's like for you, then when they try to help, it can easily feel like they're nagging you. The nagging I'm talking about here is where they keep checking up on you, but don't offer much practical support. Usually it involves a lot of 'have you...?' and 'you should...'.

Some students I coach have the completely opposite problem. Their parents couldn't care less about how well they're doing at school and show no interest at all.

Having indifferent parents is stressful but also, thankfully, rare. Most students I work with have parents who care about their education a lot and the concern can seem like nagging.

Understand your parents' point of view
One thing about parents that can sometimes be infuriating is that they really worry about you.

If you think about it, though, you never knew yourself as a baby, and they did. They held you in their arms when you were tiny and vulnerable, and they fervently hoped that you would have a better life than them. They hoped you wouldn't have to go through any of the negative experiences they did. Parents want to protect their children and want them to have a good life.

Your parents love you and they want the best for you, but it's sometimes difficult for them to accept that you are growing up. It's easy for them to slip up and forget that you're not that little kid you once were, and so they try to help but sometimes get it wrong.

The Fear Monkey won't like it, but a conversation about the pressures in school and the help you wish you could have is a starting point towards changing things round for the better. One thing you can do is to give your parents this book to read. You might underline with a pen or highlighter the problems you find most relevant. It could help them understand you better.

If you're not communicating well with your parents, they might feel like the only thing left is to scare you with horror stories about what will happen if you fail your exams. It's similar to schools' tactics, where your teachers go on and on about your future and how bleak it will be if you don't pass.

My mam and dad still worry about me, and I'm a teacher with qualifications coming out of my ears! I mention this because I don't want to make unrealistic claims about your parents stopping the worrying or nagging. Maybe they will, maybe they won't. Yes, it's annoying, but at least can you see that it's because they care? You don't have to like it, but maybe you can understand that it's coming from a good place.

Here's what one student had to say about turning to your parents for support:

> Being children (and I'm sure this is not just me), it is difficult for us to understand where our parents are coming from, as we believe they don't understand what we are going through because they

never had to go through it, when really this is not the case. My mum and dad always say: "I wasn't born yesterday" and that's true, they weren't, and they have been through everything we have. It was probably harder for them as they didn't have modern technology or resources we have now to help them study. I also believe that getting your parents to help you is great as they've all been through it, so why not get someone with experience who you trust and love to help?

Here's what students said about this problem:
'Go for walks.'

Exam Magic says:
The simple act of moving can be helpful when you're dealing with difficult emotions. Getting some fresher air and a change of scenery can help. It won't offer a solution to the problems you're dealing with, but it may help you to cope in the short term.

I'm sorry to hear you're having family problems. The world outside of home is demanding, and when we go home, we'd like to be going to a place where we feel safe and can relax. If you haven't got that, for whatever reason, it's tough to cope with. Things can be so bad that some students may have to accept that this time around, their exams are not their highest priority, and re-sitting for exams when their home lives are more stable could be an option.

If you're determined to find a way to do your best despite the emotional difficulties, then you'll want to make the best use of the facilities at school. Teachers rarely go home when the bell rings, and school can provide a quiet space where you can forget home for a while and focus on your studies.

Try to make sure your teachers know that you need some help. If your family troubles are something you want to keep to yourself, then that's your call. I don't know enough about your situation to comment. What I *can* tell you is that no matter how bad things are, we don't make things better by blaming or being hard on ourselves about what's happening.

Relationship problems, whether they're to do with friendships or romance or family, are never caused by one person alone. Little children often blame themselves when things are difficult at home. Very young children think the whole universe revolves around them, so they also tend to assume that they are the cause of what's going on in their families, whether it's good or bad. Plus they are dependent on their parents for survival and so it feels safer to take the blame than to make their parents wrong.

Even when we're not little kids anymore, we still rely on our parents for a lot of things, and so the habit of being hard on ourselves can hang around. If this is what's happening for you, you'll probably need more support than this book can give you.

Be aware that there's a better way for you, and you'll find it over time. There is someone in your school who's responsible for helping students with problems at home. Speak to them about it.

As far as school and studying go, can you give yourself permission to focus on your work and put your family problems to the back of your mind, at least some of the time? It might be hard, or even feel impossible, but aren't there times when you don't think about your family problems, even if those times last only a moment or two? Try to distract yourself in a constructive way, and focus as much as you can on schoolwork.

Even a little focus on your work is preferable to none.

PROBLEM #4: I'D RATHER SPEND TIME WITH MY BOYFRIEND OR GIRLFRIEND

Here's what students said about this problem:
'Ditch them—exams are more important.'

Exam Magic says:
Harsh advice, and not necessarily true or very helpful, either. What's more helpful is to take a step back and evaluate the relationship.

Relationships are meant to make your life better. If you have a girlfriend or boyfriend who is making life harder for you, or if they aren't supporting you in working towards your future, is that the basis for a lasting relationship? If the relationship doesn't stand much of a chance of lasting, is it a good idea to put it before your education?

The person who loves you and whom you love wants you to be happy, right? If they love you now, does that mean they also care about your future happiness?

Do you see where we're going with this one?

If you really love each other, then you'll want to build a life together. Watch out for boyfriends and girlfriends who distract you from your studying. The better your qualifications are, the more choices you have about what you do next, after school. If you have a boyfriend or girlfriend who supports you and wants the best for you, they'll help you get better results so that you both have more choices and more freedom in the future. At least that's the rational way of looking at it.

In reality, when you're in love, it feels so good that anything which gets in the way of being together is painful. Your boyfriend or girlfriend might be a different age and might not be studying. They might want things to carry on as normal and don't want you spending more time away from them. You might worry that they could break up with you and find someone else.

This problem is difficult because when you're in love, it's a big deal. Your future is also a big deal. It deserves some thought.

Are you worried they might leave you or you could lose them?

If your boyfriend or girlfriend would leave you because you're working towards your future, is that the kind of person you have a future with?

Think about it for a moment. What have you noticed about the people you know? If someone is sort of selfish and doesn't listen, do they keep on behaving like that? If you are letting your boyfriend or girlfriend hold you back from investing in your future, it'll probably keep happening.

You might not want to study and might prefer to spend your time hanging out with your boyfriend or girlfriend. That's certainly a lot more fun, but how do you think you'll feel about each other if one of you knows they allowed the other one to hold them back? You might start to resent or mistrust each other. Resentment and distrust are poison to relationships. They have a way of eating away at the sunshine until only grey clouds are left.

You must find ways to prepare for your exams if you want to be successful in passing them. Make sure you're not using your boyfriend or girlfriend as a cover-up for the fear we all experience when faced with a challenge. Using people is not a very loving thing to do.

If they really love you and want to be with you in the future, they'll do whatever they can to support you now.

PROBLEM #5: I HAVE DUTIES AT HOME THAT TAKE UP MY TIME

Here's what students said about this problem:
'Prioritise.'

Exam Magic says:
I have a friend whose mum threw out all of his school and exam-prep books because he'd left them lying around on the floor of his bedroom. I remember him picking his books out of the rubbish bin in the back yard. His mum was very house proud, and a tidy house was a higher priority for her than my friend's exam results. Maybe she did it to teach him a lesson.

What I take from this incident is that we can't expect other people to respect what's important to us unless we let them know about it. Even then, they might not be able to accept it. Other things might come higher up on their list of priorities, but it's still up to us to be as clear as we can about what matters most to us.

Communication issues aside, you might find it helpful to assess your obligations. Home duties can range from washing the dishes to working in the family business to being the main carer for the family. Having a few simple chores to do would be at one end of the scale, and being the main carer at home would be at the other.

If the scale was numbered from zero to ten, where zero is no chores and ten is responsible for nearly everything, where would you score on that scale?

If you score below three or four, then maybe you'll need to look at where you're wasting time. Cut out the time-wasting and you'll have plenty of opportunities to get your work done.

If you score five or more, then you are juggling home responsibilities with the demands of school and there's a lot on your shoulders. Is it possible to ask your parents and siblings to take some of your responsibilities off your hands, at least while you study for exams? How many of the things you're in charge of could be done by someone else?

If your family is relying on you a lot, you might find the idea of putting your needs first difficult. This will be especially so if you've got used to being the one who looks after everyone else. One of your biggest challenges will be to put your own needs first even if it feels strange or you feel uncomfortable with it.

Whatever you do, don't give up or cover things over. The school is there to support you—but don't expect people to be able to read your mind and know what you need. Schools are busy places; there's so much going on, you have to step up and ask for the help you need.

Try to remember that teachers become teachers to help people. Find an approachable teacher and tell them what your problem is. You probably know who that person is already. They'll help you work out a plan.

If you're not ready or don't want to speak to anyone about it, you might want to consider that you deserve to come first at least some of the time.

PROBLEM #6: MY PARENTS COMPARE ME TO MY BROTHERS AND SISTERS

Here's what students said about this problem:
'Have a diary to record your thoughts and feelings.'

Exam Magic says:
Our Fear Monkeys don't like to be ignored. The more we ignore them, the more resourceful they get at winning our attention. You might find that your Fear Monkey decides you're taking it seriously if you record your worry thoughts in a book. This method has worked for many of the people I've coached. It could work for you, too.

Writing thoughts down is one way of acknowledging them.

Have you heard the phrase 'what we resist, persists'? It means that if we try *not* to think something, the very act of trying not to think about it makes it stronger in our minds. If we write down the thoughts in a book, somewhere private, we can put them to one side long enough to focus on something else.

It's better to have a private diary than to post your worries on social media. You want to take a break from worrying, not start a conversation about it. Talking about problems is something I'm recommending over and over again in this book, but using a diary is a different strategy. It's something you can use to get your mind off of worry thoughts and onto your studies.

Understand what's behind the comparisons
Another thing that might help you deal with the comparisons is to consider what your parents' intentions might be.

Comparing can go in one of three ways, two of which are not terribly productive. We can compare ourselves with someone who's doing better than us and feel bad, or we can compare ourselves with someone we're doing better than and feel good. The third alternative is to become inspired by someone else's achievements and strive to be more like that person.

That last option is the one your parents are aiming for, but unfortunately their method is backfiring.

To feel inspired, we have to believe in our abilities. If we think that we'll never be able to do something as well as the person we're being compared to, we feel hopeless. Hopeless is not a motivating emotional state to be in—and it's not what your parents want for you.

We rarely mean to act in ways and say things that cause the people we love to feel unhappy, but we all do it, don't we? So, what's going on when your parents compare you unfavourably to your siblings? What your parents are hoping for is that by asking why you can't be like your brother, sister, cousin, etc., they'll motivate you to change your ways and improve your results. Why do they want you to get better results in school? Ultimately it's because they worry about you and want you to be happy, safe and secure.

A more useful conversation can occur if you ask your parents to really listen to you and then tell them what frightens, stresses or confuses you about school and exams. Talking openly and honestly about emotional things might be awkward, but if you want your parents to stop comparing you to others, guess who's going to have to start that conversation?

Can you see how your parents might be trying to protect you with their comparing?

If they're hoping to inspire you to make extra effort in your exams, there are more helpful ways of going about it. Each one of us is unique, so we can't be like anyone else. We can only be ourselves.

My guess is, they just want you to be okay. Can you forgive them for that? Maybe it's too much to forgive them right now, but can you see that they're probably trying to make sure that you have a better life than them?

It's a big ask to turn things around like this. What's even harder is that they might keep on comparing, even if you are brave enough to talk about it. Life's like that—it's often unfair—but learning to respond to unfairness in constructive ways is part of growing up. It's a strength we can develop as we become more mature.

You could underline the parts of this section you agree with and give it to your parents to read. It might get the conversation started.

Problem #7: There's no quiet space to work in at home

Here's what students said about this problem:
'Work in the library—find a quiet space.'

Exam Magic says:
It's easy enough to get distracted from studying even if you do have a quiet space, and if you can't get any peace at home, you'll have to look elsewhere. Before you do that, though, have you tried asking your parents to help you create some quietness at home?

Many students have siblings to take care of or share a room. If this applies to you, is it possible to negotiate some time when you have the room to yourself, free from distractions?

If home is not the answer, then you'll need to find another space to work in. I've coached students who found it easier to work in a local café rather than at home. Other students have worked at friends' houses. Though you might have to work out some transport issues, other obvious alternatives are the public library or the school library, or a classroom where a teacher is willing to supervise you. There are after-school and lunchtime study clubs in most schools. If your school doesn't have one, ask for one to be started.

As with most problems, I suggest you work out a solution with the help of your teachers. Which teacher do you think will help you? Make a commitment to speak to them as soon as you can.

Not having a quiet space at home is a genuine problem, but don't let it stop you.

Can you find places and times where you can work? Your solution doesn't have to be perfect; it only needs to be better than the way things are now.

Here's what students said about this problem:
'Continue even if it makes you feel uncomfortable.'

Exam Magic says:
Feeling uncomfortable is necessary if you're going to face fear, grow as a person, and improve your exam results. We all get tempted to keep hitting the snooze button, but eventually we have to get out of bed and face the things we'd rather not.

It's true that learning something that interests us is much easier than struggling with a subject that doesn't. It's also true that we all have things in our lives that maybe we don't like, but we've got to do them anyway. For example, some of your subjects might actually be stepping stones to something else, in which case you still need them so you can move on.

Let me ask a question: How well are you doing in the subjects you find boring? If you are bored but doing the work, understanding the learning and getting good test results, then you don't have such a big problem as far as passing your exams is concerned. You'll get the results you need and you'll be okay.

In situations like this, can you set yourself goals that challenge you? Why not work out what it will take for you to get the highest grades possible in the subject? Maybe you could extend your studies outside of the classroom and find expert teachers online who can ignite your passion for the subject. If you seriously can't find a way to get excited about a problem subject, at least you can acknowledge that not all problems are equal. Not being challenged by the subject is a better class of problem to have than falling behind because you can't understand the work

But if the boredom has more to do with feeling left behind or being unable to do what's asked of you, what then?

Identify what's behind the boredom and discomfort
Before you can solve this problem, you might need to analyse it so you know where the boredom and discomfort are coming from. For example:

- Are you struggling with the subject matter and interpreting that feeling as boredom? Some students struggle because they've missed lessons that taught essential skills without which they can't keep up. Even if you haven't missed lessons, you might find that some subjects just take more work to understand.

- Are you tuning out and letting your thoughts wander because the teacher's style doesn't work for you?
- Are you just not interested in the subject and not seeing how you'll use it in the future?

Let's work our way through that list.

Identify options for handling the problem

Once you know what's going on, you can identify some options for meeting the challenge:

- If you're having trouble understanding the subject matter, see if you can get the help you need from the teacher of that class or from a tutor or from videos online. What will help you here is to improve your level of skill in the subject. If you think you can't grow your skills, think again. Modern research tells us that our brains can adapt and grow to develop new abilities and skills if we become determined to find a way. The quickest way to get better at something is to find a good teacher. Thankfully, today, amazing teachers are just an Internet page away!
- If your teacher's style isn't working for you, you can find a teacher online whose style suits you better. There was a time when the only teachers we had access to were the ones in our school or local area. Now you can be taught by any teacher in the world through the Internet, just by entering the subject you're studying into a search engine.

Have you looked at some of the educational videos on YouTube, for example?

- If the subject is one you have no interest in, and you are genuinely, bone-achingly, mind-numbingly bored in your lessons, you can still turn this to your advantage. I promise you, no matter what career or profession you get into, there will be tasks to face that you just don't like. Successful musicians have to spend hours waiting around to go on stage. Actors have to get up in the early hours to get on set and have their makeup done or endure endless media interviews. Millionaire business owners have to spend hours on the nitty-gritty work of keeping customers and finding new ones. You also need to learn how to make yourself do the things you don't want to do to get what you want. Your Fear Monkey will try to hold you back. It feels uncomfortable getting past the Fear Monkey and through the fear barrier, but you can do it if you decide to.

Think about what you might need to do differently

How have you been doing in your efforts to solve this problem? Are you ploughing ahead or do you feel stuck? Do you need help or just an attitude adjustment (or both)?

If you're feeling stuck, then break your tasks down into very small actions. Even if all you do today is get your class notes out of wherever they are now and walk around with them in your hand for five minutes, it's better than doing nothing. Seriously, do something every day. Even if it feels like it isn't enough, it is better than doing nothing. Our Fear Monkeys try to keep us safe by staying still.

Nobody really stands still, though. We need to keep moving because everything else is moving. If we stay still, we actually start slipping backwards compared to everyone else. This is especially true when it comes to exams. So commit to a few small actions; no matter how small they seem to you, write them down and do them. You'll feel at least a little bit better if you take action.

Are you giving up on subjects you find difficult? It can feel uncomfortable when we're faced with something that's hard to understand, or when we feel like we're not very good at something. Feeling uncomfortable and feeling bored are quite similar feelings when you think about it.

If you were certain you'd get a good exam result in the subjects that bore you, would you still find them as dull? Maybe so, but how can anything good come from giving up on a challenge?

Whenever we're faced with something we can't do and we stick to it, breaking it down into smaller and smaller pieces, our brains develop the ability to do that thing. Research tells us that intelligence and talent don't make as much of a difference as we might assume. The one deciding factor is our willingness to persist and keep working out how to do it. It is hard to keep practicing in this way, which is probably why so few people do it. If it were easy, everyone would keep going until they got exactly what they wanted—but then, not everyone knows about the Fear Monkey.

One of the things the Fear Monkey says is, 'This is hard, so best leave it till...'. Often it says 'leave it until later', but what it really wants to do is get us to give up trying and stay where it thinks we are safe, in our familiar zones. Solving the problems you're having in class is going to involve dealing with your Fear Monkey. It's going to be uncomfortable having conversations with teachers and being as open as you can, but if you don't talk with someone about the problems you're having, things are unlikely to change for the better.

It's important that you begin to look for constructive ways to make the situation better for yourself. Whatever you do, one thing is sure: finding your subjects boring is a big challenge. Life is full of challenges and as we learn to face challenges and find ways around them or under them or through them, we grow as people.

You might feel like you've tried everything, but have you really?

Are you avoiding the challenges in front of you and indulging yourself in easy activities like watching TV or browsing online?

If we let challenges stop us, then we feel stuck and that's an uncomfortable feeling. Challenges don't go away on their own, and they tend to keep on showing up in different ways. It's when we find the courage to face the things we find uncomfortable that we usually feel at least a bit better.

A student of mine, whom I'll call Denise, always tried to avoid doing any kind of work in my lessons. Then in year 10, she took the Exam Magic GCSE course and things started to change for her. I was on duty in the playground one day and I asked her how things were going.

'Oh, great, sir,' she said. 'I just got an A in my science test and I'm doing well in all of my subjects. I'm even getting on with my parents!'

Last time I knew anything about it, she was failing every test and was in trouble for bunking lessons! It surprised me so much that I had to ask her what had changed. After all, when she was in years 7, 8 and 9, she'd been in trouble with nearly all of her teachers for messing about and wasting time.

'It was when you showed us that TFAR thing, sir. Before that, I just thought I couldn't do it, so I didn't want to try, but when you said we could start with changing our thoughts, I just thought maybe I can do it.'

TFAR is part of the Exam Magic GCSE course. It's a model students use to change their minds about what they can achieve. Denise used the TFAR model to understand that if she started to think about school in a different way, she could change her results.

The TFAR model demonstrates how changes in thinking lead to changes in results. Let's work through the model, going from the R to the T, even though that might seem backwards:

- The 'R' stands for 'results'—in this case, exam results—and 'A' stands for 'actions'. The more successful actions you take towards preparing for exams, the better chance you have of getting good results.

- The 'F' stands for 'feelings'. You are motivated to move towards something you think will make you feel good, and away from something that feels bad. It's your feelings that cause your actions, and your actions that cause your results.
- The 'T' in TFAR stands for 'thoughts'. When you think a happy thought, you feel better than when you think an unhappy thought.

So, thoughts cause feelings; feelings cause actions; and actions cause results. When we want to change our results, TFAR shows us that changing our thinking is a great place to start.

Where we can go wrong is thinking about the results we want as if we can't have them. This has a negative effect on both our actions and our results.

Our thoughts, feelings and actions, along with our beliefs, make up our attitudes. When we change our attitudes, we get different results. There's a very clear logic to it when you look at it with an open mind.

Denise learned to think about the results she wanted in a way that helped her believe in her ability to achieve them. This whole book is full of advice on how to change what you think, feel and believe about yourself and school.

Another thing you can do is show this chapter to a teacher and use it to start a conversation. No matter what your Fear Monkey says about it, teachers are there to help you. Maybe this conversation will feel uncomfortable to begin with, but then, aren't you uncomfortable and bored now, struggling with things and wasting your time?

PROBLEM #9: I HAVE TOO MUCH HOMEWORK—I DON'T HAVE TIME FOR EXAM PREP

Here's what students said about this problem:
'Either you don't spend some time making a timetable and you continue to study badly, or you take out just a bit of time to make a plan you can stick to; it's worth the time.'

Exam Magic says:
Your school should run a session where they teach you how to make a study plan. If you don't get that session or you missed it, talk to your tutor and find out how to get it.

The main thing to remember here is that trying to keep everything in your head is a very ineffective way to go about things. There are very few people alive who can organise themselves without writing things down. You need some kind of written plan.

How to avoid feeling overloaded

How often do you find that your teachers all set similar deadlines for work they want handed in, so you feel like you have too much to do at once? It's a problem a lot of students talk about. Most schools in the UK should have a homework schedule in place so that the load is spread out across the week, but sometimes the assignments all seem to be due at once. It's even harder if you're behind with work and trying to catch up, and it's especially difficult as the exams get closer.

It's no fun feeling overloaded with work—nobody likes it—but most of us have to deal with it sometimes. So what do you do about it? Make a study plan, use the List & Persist method (discussed in the next section) and ask for help. (A study plan isn't the same thing as the List & Persist method; the two go together. The List & Persist method, once you get the hang of it, takes only about five minutes a day to do.)

Make a study plan

Your teachers live with the feeling of being overloaded with work nearly all of the time. The ones who handle it really well are good ones to ask for help. How do you spot teachers who handle pressure well? They are the ones who know what your marks are, remember your name, don't lose your coursework and are fair and cheerful most, if not all, of the time. If you ask one of these teachers how they keep on top of everything, they'll tell you they don't, and they often feel as if things are slipping out of control. What they do about it is to prioritise. They'll tell you that it's very important to prioritise your activities and schedule how you use your time. In other words, you need a timetable that splits your time between homework, study time and social and relaxing time.

If you try holding everything in your head, you'll drive yourself up the wall. Things we hold in our minds tend to grow. If we hold a problem in mind without taking action to solve it, the problem will appear to get bigger and bigger until doing anything about it seems impossible. You've absolutely got to write your workload down and plan how you'll tackle it.

There's no way around it. Maybe you won't get everything done, but it's better to get some of it done rather than none. Holding it in your head, with no plan of action, usually ends up with very little work getting done and a lot of time wasted in either trying to forget about it or trying to remember it all. It can even drive you towards giving up altogether!

Writing a plan doesn't have to be complicated or difficult. In fact, you should use the simplest method possible because that will mean you actually use it!

List & Persist

Use the List & Persist method
One way to organise your work is to use the List & Persist method. Here's how it works: Keep a notebook or pad by your bed. Each night before you go to sleep, write down five or six things that absolutely must get done the next day. Then ask yourself, if only one of those things got done, which one would be most important? Number it #1.

Then ask the same question about the remaining unnumbered tasks. If you did only one of those remaining, which one would be most important? That's number #2, and so on, until all of the tasks are numbered in decreasing order of importance.

You can tweak this method so that it works for you. Maybe you'll have fewer items on your list, maybe you'll struggle to know how to number them, but you'll find a way that works. Include the clubs and societies and social events that are important, too. You're not a machine. You need a life, but you also need a plan. Forget about doing it perfectly; just do it your way. That'll be good enough to start.

Write your list before you go to sleep and look at it when you wake up. Do item #1 as soon as you can. When it's done, tick it off. If you don't do an item, put an arrow next to it and put it on your list for tomorrow.

There's a reason I'm telling you to look at your list just before you go to sleep. Have you ever heard the phrase 'Let me sleep on it'? When you make your list the last thing you look at before you sleep, your subconscious mind, which never switches off, works on your list while your conscious mind is sleeping, and your subconscious mind will help you figure out the best way to get as much done in the best way possible when you wake up.

If you're hearing about your subconscious mind for the first time and don't get it, don't worry about it. The Exam Magic GCSE course will help you understand more about it. What's important is that you start a plan. The List & Persist method is one relatively straightforward and highly effective way to get organised.

Ask for help

If you still feel overwhelmed with homework and exam prep, have a quiet word with a teacher. Go to them at break time or lunch or after school and tell them about your situation.

Before you see them, make a list of the problems you're struggling with. It doesn't have to be anything complicated; just a few sentences on a piece of paper will help you organise your thoughts.

Maybe you don't have a study timetable, or you might have a list of assignments you are behind with and you can't see a way to catch up. Whatever the problem is, it might seem impossible to you, but remember that teachers are specially trained to help people with their studies. They've been through the process you're going through now and will be able to help you, but the first move is up to you.

If it's uncomfortable for you to do this, don't let the Fear Monkey stop you from getting the help you need.

Problem #10: I don't have the right notes or resources

Here's what students said about this problem:
'Use YouTube teaching channels and online workbooks.'

Exam Magic says:
If you type any subject into the Search box on YouTube, you'll come up with loads of videos. It's a fast and free way to get help. Your school might have a subscription to exam-prep websites, and there are also free ones. You can search for them and find one that you like the look of. You'll need a list of topics so you can keep track of what you're covering and find the right resources.

You can also go into most bookstores and buy study

guides. You can get them second-hand on eBay. You can borrow them from the school or public library. The problem isn't getting your hands on the material; it's knowing what to look for and organising your time.

Here's what else students said about this problem:
'Ask teachers what to study.'

Exam Magic says:
Will talking to a teacher and letting them know you've not got it together feel awkward? As exam time gets closer and closer, teachers are under more and more pressure and you might run the risk of having them respond with less than a joyful attitude, but it will be more to do with the situation than anything to do with you.

As teachers, we are responsible for making sure you have the fairest chance of success. Make a list of subjects you have missing notes for and start a conversation to help sort it out. If you do this, someone will help you. I won't say 'Don't be embarrassed', because you probably will feel uncomfortable doing this. Teachers might give you a hard time about it, especially if they're stressed, but they shouldn't reject you and refuse to help. I'd hope there'd be some teachers who'd be happy about your taking the initiative.

Ask for help now, today, as soon as you can walk into a classroom, and let out the truth. Remind yourself that your teachers are part of the team helping you get the best results possible. Be brave, drop the excuses, face what's in front of you. Can you afford to let your Fear Monkey stop you?

This problem needs immediate attention. If you leave it any longer, you're going to be really stuck.

Your school is bursting at the seams with notes and books and other resources with content you need to know for each of your subjects. All it takes to get your hands on those resources is time, the will and the courage to do it, plus maybe a little humility on your part.

You can ask to photocopy other people's notes. You can borrow or buy study guides. You can find online study guides and ask how to get access to a computer if you don't have one. There is so much help available to you nowadays that the only thing that can get between you and it is your discomfort about asking for or admitting that you need help. In other words, Fear Monkey stuff.

Try not to listen to the tricks, fantasies and excuses your Fear Monkey comes up with. It will be okay if you take action and do something about it. Excuses only make things worse.

Do you know the only thing worse than an excuse?

A good excuse!

Here's what students said about this problem:
'It's better to speak to teachers at lunch, during a break or after school about problems, than to argue in class. If you can at least tell them what's wrong with their lesson, maybe they can do something to change it!"

And:

'Liking yourself is more important than liking your teachers.'

Exam Magic says:
Have you ever been in class when someone starts arguing with the teacher, maybe shouting and getting angry? Hopefully it doesn't happen a lot in your school, but when it does, it's almost impossible for the issue to

get sorted out with everyone watching. If the student isn't able to calm down, they'll usually be asked to leave the room, and then later the teacher and student can work through the conflict without an audience. It's easier to talk without the rest of your class watching and listening to every word.

Shouting and slamming doors is one extreme example of not getting on with a teacher. Sometimes students don't try as hard in a subject if they don't like the teacher. They might turn up late or even miss classes. The desire to avoid people we don't like is quite natural, but when your exam scores are at stake, is it the right thing for you?

Remember why you're doing all this

If you have a teacher whom you get on with and respect, and who you believe cares about how well you do in their subject, does that make you more motivated? Most people would answer yes. If you feel like your teacher is disrespecting you or isn't bothered whether you do well or not, or if you find them rude, it can have the opposite effect. Not wanting to do your work because you don't like the teacher is an easy mistake to make, but it is still a mistake!

You're not working for your teachers. You're working for your future.

The better your grades and qualifications are, the more choices you have about the future. Damaging your future because you don't like your teacher is an emotional thing to do. It's understandable, but it's not logical.

Be clear about your priorities

All schools have rules, and most of them make sense from the point of view of making sure that everyone respects everyone else's right to learn. Teachers enforce the rules, but you might not agree with every single rule, right? In my school, one of my highest-achieving students just happened also to enjoy colouring her hair bright pink. When the school decided to make a rule saying bright pink wasn't okay and hair had to be natural shades only, she and her parents had choices to make. Clearly the colour of her hair had nothing to do with her scores, but to complain or protest about it would have distracted her from her main goal, which was to do the best thing for her future. She complained about it a bit, changed the colour of her hair and got on with her studies.

Maybe you don't like your teachers because they enforce the school rules. If that's the case, my question to you is: 'Are you doing the right thing?' Are you respecting your right to learn and the rights of the other people in your school?

Maybe what you dislike is the *way* a teacher enforces the rules, but aren't there other students in your class who feel the same way, but respond differently? My guess is that they've set doing well as a higher priority than whether they like or agree with their teacher.

You, too, need to get clear on what your priorities are right now. I'm not suggesting that you agree with injustice, but I do urge you to be honest with yourself. Sometimes our Fear Monkeys will try to distract us rather than have us face the difficult business of studying and expanding our familiar zones.

See what's coming

My good friend and brilliant colleague Sherife Tayfun is a pioneer in teaching students how to mentor each other. One thing she has students do is think ahead and see what's coming. For example, one student—we'll call him Aaron—would often get into disagreements with teachers, and that wasted a lot of his time and energy as well as the school's. One time he forgot his PE kit and came to Sherife in a terrible mood. He didn't want to go to his PE lesson because it made him angry just thinking about getting told off for forgetting his kit. The background was that Aaron's mum was having some problems coping and Aaron was moving from one relative's home to another and that's why he didn't have the right PE equipment. He didn't want his personal circumstances discussed in front of everyone.

Sherife had Aaron think ahead. What would happen when he got to his lesson? The teacher would tell him off. Then what would happen? He'd have to get some school PE kit from the laundry. Then what? He'd get on with the lesson, looking a bit silly in the borrowed PE kit.

When Aaron looked ahead in his mind, it helped him avoid flying off the handle when he saw his teacher. Can you think of a situation where you might use this same approach?

Think about what you're bringing with you

Students tell me that if they have a grumpy or annoying start at home, it can affect their whole day. By the time they get to school and bump into their least favourite teacher, it can be very tempting to take the whole thing out on them. Sometimes it's easier to blame someone other than the person we're actually upset or angry with. Could this scenario apply to any of the situations you sometimes find yourself in?

When we're emotionally wound up, knowing what's best for us can be hard. Teachers struggle with emotions, too. Did you ever see your teacher in the street and get a surprise, like you kind of expected them to exist only in school? Teachers also have friends and families and worries not directly related to school.

It might be that a run-in with a teacher had a lot to do with problems you were both experiencing with other people. If that's the case, how does that change the way you think about things?

If you really feel like a teacher doesn't care about you, couldn't that make you want to prove them wrong?

I remember one student telling me that her English teacher had told her that she just wasn't a very creative person and that her creative writing would probably never be very good. The student's attitude was that it's not her teacher's place to decide how creative she is.

She didn't even want to prove her teacher wrong. She decided to prove to herself that she could write and that she'd write the way she wanted, and that would be good enough for her. She got motivated to do her best and she looked for help from friends and other teachers. She took an Exam Magic Course, changed her mind about what she could achieve and passed her English GCSE!

The only person any of us needs to prove anything to is ourselves.

Maybe you're not feeling as brave as my student was, but at least be very clear that you're not working for your teachers. You're working for you!

If your own teacher feels unapproachable, then you could go to a different teacher of that subject or to the head of that department and speak to them for some advice. You may also find it helpful to study with friends in a group. Doing that might help other students feel less alone in their struggles, too.

Here's what students said about this problem:
'Think about why you're doing this.'

Exam Magic says:
Be aware that we always have choices. Which choices will work out best for you? The better the choices we make, the better our experiences turn out. It's logical. Where it can get confusing is when our emotions cloud our thinking.

School can be a very pressured place. It's not just your teachers who pile the pressure on; it can also come from parents, friends, siblings, and wider family and from comparing yourself to others. It feels bad to be compared to someone or some standard and not to measure up. (For help with those issues, see the strategies suggested for Problem #1 and Problem #6.)

Feeling pressured all the time can drain your motivation to work hard in school and affect the way you make decisions, so it's important to understand how motivation works. There are two basic types of human motivation—negative and positive—and schools generally rely a lot on the first type to make sure everyone keeps doing the right thing.

Schools in the UK hold assemblies with countdowns to the number of weeks until exam time, and the consequences of failing your exams or of getting poor results are made graphically clear. Add in the sanctions you get for not following rules, and teachers telling you what to do, and it's easy to see why this approach could be considered to be nagging.

It's actually negative motivation. Negative motivation means that you're doing your best to avoid pain or discomfort.

For example, imagine that you're on a bus and you don't pay attention to where you're sitting, and you begin to realise that the person next to you has a body odour issue. Not only that, but they're also gradually taking up more and more of the seat and are using their phone to play music you find unpleasant. You'll be motivated to get up and change seats because you want to get away from the unpleasant smells and sounds and stop the invasion of your personal space.

Although negative motivation can be effective, relying on it too much of the time can feel bad. Are you getting countdowns from your teachers about how many more weeks are left until your exams? Have you been told what a nightmare your life will be if you fail your exams? It's all negative. It doesn't feel nice, but if you were positively motivated, you'd need less of it.

When you're positively motivated, it means that you're moving towards a more pleasant experience. For example, if you're thirsty and there's a glass of water in front of you, you pick up the glass and take a drink. You're motivated to take action because you think you'll feel better when you've drunk some water.

Decide which scores you want to get

If you take the Exam Magic GCSE course at school, you will experience how it feels to pass exams with the results you really want, and you'll get this experience by doing an exercise called the Results Role Play. It gives you a chance to find some positive motivation. Can you begin to imagine yourself with the exam results you want? Take a moment to do this exercise. You can use the space below to write your subjects and best possible results. Setting goals in this way is one step towards getting positively motivated.

In the first column, titled 'Exam Subjects', write a list of all the subjects you will take exams in. In the second column, titled 'Best Results', write down the best grade or result you've ever got in that subject, or if you don't know what that is, guess what you think you can get if you work as hard as you can.

In the third column, write a grade or number that is one higher than each of those you wrote in column 2. It has to be a whole grade higher. It can't be a plus or a minus, because you won't get plus or minus scores in your final results. If you have C in column 2, write B in column 3. If you have B+ in column 2, you can write either A or A+ in column 3. If you're in the UK you'll be using numbers as grades. In that case you should go two numbers higher in the third column so that 3 becomes 5 and 4 becomes 6 and so on.

The results in column 3 are your goals for each subject. A goal is always at least one step beyond what you know how to do now. Working towards goals we've set for ourselves can be motivating, so do the exercise now.

Exam Subjects	Best Results	Goals

If you positively motivate yourself, you'll get less nagging from your teachers and parents. If they keep nagging you even when you think you're doing everything you possibly can, show them the grades you're working towards and ask them to help you achieve them.

Maybe they will be able to help you find ways of doing it better. Exams are something you take on your own, but you don't pass them on your own. Your school can provide you with the support and resources you need to get the results you want.

PROBLEM #13: I PREFER TO MESS AROUND OR CHAT WITH MY FRIENDS

Here's what students said about this problem:
'Leave out the banter.'

Exam Magic says:
We've pretty much covered this one. You've got to have fun, but not at the expense of your education.

If messing around in class has anything to do with your feeling like it's not worth bothering or that you can't do it, then leaving out the banter might be good advice for you. If you carry on messing around in class, you will definitely get worse exam results than you're capable of.

In every class you take, you're being asked for something. There are exercises to complete, information to learn and analyse, questions to answer and maybe things to make. If you believe that you can't do what's being asked of you, it can feel safer to chat with friends and distract yourself rather than admit you're struggling. Maybe you have friends in class who distract you?

Either way, if you're not feeling good about your abilities, your Fear Monkey will look for other ways to feel good or get approval or feel popular. You could even do a very good job of fooling yourself into believing that school doesn't matter, or at least that it's okay to avoid doing the work in front of you.

One student I coached wanted to be a professional rugby player when he left school. He already had trials with a team and was accepted into their training programme. He didn't think it was worth concentrating in the classes he found difficult, and he was distracting his friends, too. I asked him if he'd ever have to face challenges as he built his rugby career. He had to admit that he would. He'd be training with players who might be a lot stronger or fitter or skilled than he was. There would be pressures to perform and decisions to be made about transferring to other teams and managing his finances.

We meet challenges by being brave and sticking with them, especially when we feel nervous or we're afraid we'll mess up. The way you meet one challenge tends to set the pattern for the way you meet most of the difficult things in life.

If you are messing around or chatting in class, you can start to change things by acknowledging why you're doing it.

If you've got a reputation for messing around, changing your behaviour will feel risky. People will obviously notice the change and might judge you for it. If your popularity has anything to do with being a class clown or rebel, are you willing to change and put your future first? What would others think about you then?

What's the worst thing that can happen if you face the challenges in front of you and fail?

You'll know that you could've done better if you'd started studying earlier and worked more consistently. That's better than kidding yourself that it doesn't matter. If all you learn is to kid yourself, then you'll probably keep on kidding yourself until something really serious comes along to change your mind.

Isn't it better to face up to the truth now?

Often when I'm coaching students through their exams, one of the things they know they need to do is ask their teachers to seat them away from their friends in class. It's better to get the teacher to do this to avoid any potential embarrassment. You probably already know whom you need to be moved away from and in which class. Have the conversation as soon as possible; the less time you waste in lessons, the less time you need to spend catching up out of lessons.

Blaming your friends for distracting you can be a handy way of covering up that you're struggling with the work and want to avoid it. You care enough about your exams to be reading this guide, though, and you're looking for ways to change things. Most of the suggestions you're finding here aren't easy things to do.

It takes courage and focus to overcome a challenge. Developing more courage and focus is something we can all do that serves us well for the rest of our lives.

Keep reminding yourself that you are working for your future. It's about you growing as a person and living a life that you choose. Can you afford to let other people choose for you? You certainly don't want your Fear Monkey doing the choosing. Even your very best friends don't care about your future as much as they care about their own, because they're not you. They've got their own Fear Monkeys to deal with.

Your friends won't take your exams for you, or earn your living, or live your life.

If you continue to think that life happens to you and you have no choices, it'll keep on happening like that—but it doesn't have to be that way. If you do choose to continue to be distracted in class and to chat, at least be responsible enough to make sure you don't distract other students who are trying their best.

Even better: why not join them and try to change things? We all have to start taking responsibility for ourselves sooner or later. The sooner we do it, the better.

PROBLEM #14: I'VE GOT OUT-OF-SCHOOL CLUBS AND SPORTS THAT ARE IMPORTANT TO ME

Here's what students said about this problem:
'Split time between school, studying, and social activities.'

Exam Magic says:
You're human, so your study plan and the List & Persist method ought to take this into account. Yes, exams take priority, especially as you get closer to them, but you also have other things that are important to you. Estimate how effective you're being with your time, and drop the stuff that's a complete waste of time.

No one is suggesting that you have no time to yourself or that you work from the minute you wake up to the minute you fall asleep. Physical exercise aids concentration, and your study plan needs to factor in the sports and leisure activities that help you stay in good physical and emotional balance. What's sensible is to look at the amount of time you're throwing away on things that are not helping you get the best out of your time.

I ask students to use a scale of zero to ten, where ten is using their time 100 percent effectively and zero is completely wasting it, all of the time. Someone who is a few months away from their exams and who estimates that they are at eight out of ten on the scale is roughly on track because they are using their time 80 percent effectively. If someone says they are at four out of ten, they've got a problem because they are using their time only 40 percent effectively.

What's your score? How are you using your most precious non-renewable resource? Anyone scoring four or less out of ten is wasting 60 percent or more of their time.

Sports and school clubs don't count as time wasted. It's the amount of time spent texting, or on social media, or playing video games or... well, you know how you waste your time.

The time for your essential activities is found by taking it from stuff that's frivolous and no help whatsoever in helping you focus on your priorities. If you're not wasting time on frivolous activities and you're still short on time, then maybe you will have to make some short-term sacrifices in terms of clubs and societies.

PROBLEM #15: I CAN'T BE BOTHERED

Here's what students said about this problem:
'Leave it for a while, relax, and come back to it later.'

Exam Magic says:
When someone says 'I can't be bothered', they may be asking, 'What's the point?' or they could be feeling overwhelmed and don't believe they can do anything about all of the things being asked of them. Does this apply to you? Are you feeling like you just want to hide or go to sleep?

It's natural to go through emotional ups and downs, and maybe once in a while what you need is to snuggle yourself away someplace warm and cosy and give yourself a break. There are times we all need a 'duvet day'.

But what if feeling like you can't cope is something very familiar that you're experiencing often, maybe even every day? When we're feeling hopeless or demotivated, what helps is to find ways to see things from a different angle or point of view.

School suits some people better than others, and there are, and maybe always will be, intelligent people who learn in school to believe that they're failing. It could be that they don't learn well by sitting still and doing reading- and writing-based tasks. If you look around in the world, you'll see that there's a lot more to life than what goes on in a classroom.

But in school, we have to become proficient at literacy and numeracy in order to get good marks. There's a lot of importance placed on getting good marks. On top of this focus on words and numbers, we're also asked to learn facts that sometimes seem completely irrelevant to our lives. Some subjects also group students according to how good their test scores are.

I wonder how much attention you give to the comments your teachers write on your work. In my experience, students ignore the comments and look straight at the grade or score. If it's a high score, they feel a sense of relief or pleasure; if it's low, then they feel bad or even feel crushed. Learning new things can be difficult. In fact, it's meant to be challenging precisely because it forces you to grow. Teachers' feedback and comments are supposed to both challenge and support you, but it's easy to feel judged.

It's hard for any of us to be motivated if we feel like we can't do something and to think that even if we did try, we'd never be good enough.

You might have very good reasons to give up. If you've ever felt embarrassed or humiliated or hopeless in school, it's understandable that you'd want to avoid feeling that way again. Maybe this doesn't perfectly describe your own situation, but do you recognise any of these things?

'I've given up, because I've lost any hope I can do this' might be a more accurate way of saying 'I can't be bothered.'

If this is anywhere near the truth for you, what can you do about it?

Show a teacher this part of the book. Use it as a way of starting a conversation. From there, you and the teacher will have a chance at working out a plan for you to begin to solve the problems you're feeling stuck with. Part of that plan will be to break down the work into manageable chunks that you can handle, one step after the other.

See if you can imagine how it would feel if you were more skilled at the work you're being asked to do. Would that change things for you?

Don't get bogged down in trying to work out a complete solution to your problems. You probably won't be able to do that all in one go. One of the Fear Monkey's biggest lies is that we should give up because we can't solve our problems all at once.

Problems get solved one step at a time. The step ahead of you is a big one and asking for help will take a lot of courage. Saying you can't be bothered is much easier than facing the mixed emotions you're currently feeling about exams, yourself and school.

No-one can make you change your mind, but if you decide to try, you will find ways to make things better for yourself. Your brain is designed to find answers for you, but you have to decide to look for them. Are you ready to decide? If not now, when will you?

We all have to take responsibility for ourselves at some point in our lives. Why not do it now, when you have a team of people ready to help you work out how?

Too right; it is!

Here's what students said about this problem:
'Set certain hours for TV.' 'Watch favourite programmes on catch-up.' 'Turn off distractions.'

Exam Magic says:
Catch-up is great because you get to decide when you watch, and you can always stop a programme and come back to it later. How you will resist the temptation to veg out for too long is something you'll need to work out for yourself.

Some students get their parents to help them by giving up their devices and agreeing to times when they can use them. That can be a good start. Studying doesn't happen by itself, though, so even if your parents lock you in your room with no distractions, it's still up to you to do the work. Listening to the Audio Patch will help you build up your ability to focus.

Is it okay to watch TV? Of course it is! It's nice to relax with a favourite programme, forget our troubles and be entertained. We all love a bit of distraction and sometimes we really need to switch off and relax.

Be aware, though, that you're playing with fire when it comes to TV. The people who make TV programmes are highly skilled. They know a thing or two about capturing our attention and keeping it, and they get paid very well for doing that. The more eyeballs they attract, the better the chances they'll keep the work and the money coming in. We, on the other hand, get paid nothing for watching TV!

Anything passive generally costs us either time or money or both; have you noticed? We pay for the things we consume; we get paid for the things we create. TV shows that aren't helping you study, cost you time – time and attention are two of your most precious resources.

(If TV is your passion, then why not learn how to make TV programmes? That way you'd be putting together a plan for a successful career.)

Even watching your favourite shows on catch-up can be tricky. You know how it goes—'I'll just watch one episode' turns into another, then another and before you know it, you're going to bed too late, waking up feeling tired, and maybe starting to feel guilty or worried that time is slipping away and you're not getting anywhere with your studying. Eventually you can't even enjoy the programmes because of the nagging feeling that something's wrong.

Listen to that feeling. It's your gut telling you that your attention is being used. The people who make TV shows don't care about your future; they don't even know who you are. Limit the time you spend on them and spend more time on yourself.

Keep your priorities in mind the next time you're tempted to watch TV instead of working towards your future success. Preparing for exams is the challenge in front of you that requires both your time and your attention.

PROBLEM #17: SOCIAL NETWORKS ARE IMPORTANT TO ME AND I SPEND A LOT OF TIME ON THEM

Here's what students said about this problem:
'Turn off the Internet.'

Exam Magic says:
As with TV, try to keep in mind that unless you're making money online, you're spending rather than earning. If you invest more time in your studies, you'll get the benefit. If you invest your time and attention in social networks, that's okay, but is it taking you forward to where you want to be?

An alien from outer space looking at our species might find it strange how much time we spend looking at our phones and computers. The alien might not get just how powerfully we're drawn to belonging to groups and fitting in, maintaining our status with the people who matter to us.

By 'status' I mean where we fit in within the group. Are we in or out, high up in a group's hierarchy or low?

If you've ever been trolled, you'll know how bad being criticised or left out can feel. Being involved in a conversation and accepted by a group feels good. The opposite causes fear and anxiety.

You might have heard the term 'FOMO', short for 'fear of missing out'. We think that if we're not connected to our networks all the time, we'll miss something important. In reality, if we switched off the constant flow of updates and pictures on our social networks and came back to them after a period of studying, the stream would still be flowing. It's not actually going anywhere.

If you dip out of your networks, you'll feel a pull to take a peek and see what's happening. That's normal. The flow of information online is the perfect place to avoid facing the challenges in front of us. Personally I think it's sensible to accept that we're involved in social networks and that they mean something significant to us. However, it's equally important to accept that it's not such a great idea to cave in to the compulsion to spend time online when you know you have work that needs doing.

So what do you do about it?

If you can, switch off your browser and turn off your phone while you're studying. If you are studying online, then turn off the updates so you're not getting constant reminders every time someone does something in your networks. Messages flashing on your screens will pull your attention away from the work in front of you. That's what the messages are designed for.

We've touched on the idea that people make money from keeping other people's attention so they can sell them things. It's called the *attention economy*. This is how YouTubers make their money. The more people who pay attention to their videos, the more advertising money they earn. It's similar to TV, but it works differently because you can contribute to the conversation online in ways you can't with TV.

The point is that people are doing everything they can to get your attention. Your studies require your attention so you can earn the qualifications to move on to the next stage of your life.

Attention eats time. Time invested in study is time invested in you.

Here's what students said about this problem:
'Give up your phone for an hour.'

Exam Magic says:
You need to find a way of putting your phone away and getting on with your work. How might you do that? Can you focus for twenty minutes at a time without looking at your phone?

To work or study effectively, most of us need periods of time without distractions constantly interrupting our train of thought. You'll find it easier to ignore your phone if it is on silent and out of sight. Some students give their phones to their parents to keep hold of while they work. How you do it is up to you; experiment to see what works and then stick to it.

This problem is similar to the problem with social networks. Our phones connect us. We're emotionally attached to them and to being part of something bigger than ourselves. The draw of checking our phones can feel so strong that it's like an addiction, something we can't control.

Ask yourself a question, though. Is it true that you *can't* not check your phone, or is it more like you just don't *want* to stop? You could give it up if, instead of working for an hour, you were going shopping with a gazillion pounds to spend on anything you liked. Sure, you'd probably buy an upgraded phone, but do you get the point?

It can feel like you don't have a choice, but you actually do. Yes, it seems really hard to put your phone down and concentrate on something else, but it's not impossible. You won't have your phone with you when you take the exams, and your exams are approaching fast.

Technology pulls on our attention and plays with our need to connect, and 'digital distraction' is a problem for adults as well as for students. You'll need to decide—perhaps many times a day—whether you will let yourself be controlled by your phone or treat it as a tool you're using to make your life better.

Some students have even suggested deleting all social network apps from their phones to relieve temptation, but keeping the passwords so they can log back in after the exams are finished. That might seem too much for most. Here's one mum's advice, which may be a lot more practical:

'From experience with a phone-addicted teen, I think just putting the phone somewhere else other than where you study and leaving it there until you are done is the best approach.'

Here's what students said about this problem:
'Divide your studying into chunks.'

Exam Magic says:
If you feel that you're naturally disorganised and your room usually looks like a whirlwind has whipped all your clothes and books and whatever else, scattering them everywhere, so what? Not being organised isn't as big a problem as you might think it is. It's not as if you have to have everything totally under control, your pens and pencils labelled and stored neatly, and everything completely orderly and perfect. All you need is a space that's clear enough to sit down, a study plan, and your books and notes in one place so you can find them easily.

Start by breaking down your tasks into chunks, as my

students advised. For example, you can start with your workspace, wherever that is. You can pick up the mess on the floor and pile it in one place. You can hunt around for your books and notes and pile them in one place. You can sit down and write a list of your exam subjects. You can write the days of the week on a piece of paper and then decide which subjects you will study on which days. Now you have a place to work, the start of a plan and your books nearby.

Sometimes it feels like getting organised is too much to handle, but that's just your Fear Monkey playing its tricks on you. It's another attempt to avoid facing the fact that you actually have work to do to pass your exams.

Whenever you feel overwhelmed, keep chunking the stuff you have to do down into smaller and smaller activities, until they are so small that you actually find it ridiculous not to do them. For instance, if days are passing and you've not even opened a book, sit down and open your books for one minute. This might sound like it won't make much difference—until you realise that you're more likely to get started if you set a small task. It's a way of stepping past your Fear Monkey.

The hardest part is getting going. If you've ever push-started a car, you know that the hardest part is getting it rolling. Once it's rolling, momentum helps it keep going.

Even if all you do today, straight after reading this, is tidy up a bit, you'll feel better. You might even find that when your room or workspace is neat, you can think more clearly.

PROBLEM #20: I'VE GOT BETTER THINGS TO DO WITH MY TIME THAN STUDYING—I WANT A LIFE!

Here's what students said about this problem:
'Do important things first; then chill.'

Exam Magic says:
It's tempting to do the fun stuff first and then get around to studying later. In your experience, has this ever worked?

One episode of your favourite show leads to another, then another and before you know it, you've run out of time. It's the same with social media, phone messages, video games—you name it. Most of the stuff that eats up our attention has been designed to do exactly that. People make money from capturing other people's attention.

You need your attention focused on your priorities if you're to choose a life worthy of you.

Of course you've got more fun things to do, and yes, you want a life. Studying doesn't usually come very high on most students' lists of fun things to do, but it is very high on the list of necessary things if you want to pass your exams.

Have you made a study plan? Your plan will also have space in it for social time. Nobody is suggesting that you work without breaks. It's true that you'll have less free time as you get ready for your exams, but once they are over, you'll have the whole of the summer to do whatever you like.

You can ignore your responsibilities, but you'll pay a price. You are responsible for how this phase of your life turns out. It's one of the first major challenges you have to face. How you handle this one can have a big effect on how you face the ones that will come after it.

What do you think you'll learn to believe about yourself if you hide from the challenges of exams? Will you learn anything that you can use to meet future challenges in your work and relationships?

You don't just want a life; you want a *good* life. Our lives are made up of the decisions we make. You can decide that you're not strong enough to make yourself do the work you need to do to get the results you want. But how can a decision like that ever lead to long-term happiness? There's more at stake here than exam results.

Lives are made—they don't just happen. It's an active process of choosing to do the *right* thing for you, not the *easiest*. Imagine what kind of inner strength you'll develop if you see that you can step up and do what needs to be done.

Now is the time for tough decisions. Do you really have better things to do than laying the foundation for your future life so that you can have it the way you want it to be?

PROBLEM #21: MY SATURDAY/PART-TIME JOB TAKES A LOT OF MY TIME

Here's what students said about this problem:
'Balance your time.'

Exam Magic says:
Time, as I mentioned earlier, is one of our most precious non-renewable resources. Everyone gets twenty-four hours each day, and once time is spent, we don't get it back.

How much choice do you really have about how you use your time?

Exam season's approaching, and preparing for it is a wise investment. The work you do now towards earning your qualifications will pay off in the summer when you receive your results.

If you're spending so much time at work that your exam results are going to suffer, then the job is limiting your future choices. Remember, the better your qualifications, the more choices you have about what you do next and where you do it.

Whether you're saving up for something or helping your family or just like having money, earning it is important and every job has a learning curve to it. It feels good to have your own money and the freedom that comes with that. Can you take on extra hours at work after your exams are finished? That way you'll have better qualifications *and* more cash.

Part-time jobs are positive things, but they do have their limits. It's a balancing act. How much good are you getting now, and how much are you limiting your future?

If you're not paying rent or contributing to your family's living expenses, then the money you're getting now might seem pretty good. But if you had to start paying for food, housing, electric bills and so on, I'm guessing the money would run out pretty soon. Unless your part-time job is teaching you skills that can lead to a career in something you love, it must be thought of as a temporary thing. It is unwise to allow short-term gain to damage your long-term future chances.

Can you see yourself, or would you be happy, doing your part-time or Saturday job for the rest of your life?

It's your call. There's plenty of advice in this book about managing your time. If your parents aren't deciding how many hours you can work in your part-time job, then it's up to you to decide. That's a lot of responsibility. It's also a fact that those of us who are able to sacrifice short-term benefits for longer-term gains end up better off financially than those of us who just take the money now and fail to plan for the future.

I don't know your circumstances, so my best advice is to think about where your priorities are now, especially if you want to have a lot more money later on.

Here's what students said about this problem:
'Grow a pair!'

Exam Magic says:
Er… not the nicest way to say it, and I'm not sure how the girls are meant to take this advice, but at least it sticks in the mind. What the students mean, of course, is 'Be brave!' But let's be clear about what that advice means: being brave isn't about not being afraid; it's about being afraid and still taking action.

Fear is normal—and you can use it to your advantage
It's okay to be scared of failing. Infact fear can even be a good thing when it motivates you to study and practice to avoid failure.

Where does the idea come from that being scared is a bad thing? Think about how many people love scary movies; we actually pay to be frightened. Exams feel different because it's your real life we're talking about here, so rather than being passive, as you would be in a cinema watching someone else's life, you need to take action—especially while you are afraid.

Burn up your fear by taking action. Fear can be fuel.

Remember, the Fear Monkey tries to get you to stay still and avoid taking action because it believes it's keeping you safe. The Fear Monkey doesn't know any ways of dealing with challenges other than to run, fight or hide, but you can't run from, hide from or fight exams and still get what you want.

The worst situation you can put yourself in is to worry so much about failing that you are too frightened to do anything.

Your fear will go down at least a little bit as you get into doing the work needed to pass your exams. You stand a better chance if you're prepared.

It's okay to complain about the work for a while and get together with your friends and swap stories about how unfair and scary it is and how you wish you didn't have to do this. You can find fault with the school, your teachers, your parents and the world in general, but then you still have to do something about it.

The fear won't leave you alone until you face it by taking action. Fear isn't a weakness; it's part of the experience of being human, and we humans have Fear Monkeys to contend with.

Practice

Are you taking practice exams based on old papers under timed conditions? It's like sports training or rehearsing for a music or theatre performance. You're going to want to make your mistakes during practice so that you do the real thing the best you can.

Change the images in your mind

Do you think about the future and picture yourself failing? If you are having a hard time seeing yourself in the future with good exam results, that can cause fear, too.

The thoughts you hold in your mind cause the feelings you experience. If you see yourself failing your exams, you'll scare yourself. As discussed earlier, this isn't all bad—*if* you use the fear as fuel for action.

A better strategy is to see yourself, in your mind, having passed your exams with the results you want. This image can motivate you into action and feels better than worrying about failing.

Athletes, for example, deliberately practice this way of thinking. They see themselves doing the actions they need to do to win and they see themselves winning. It's a big part of their training. It helps them stay positive and deal with their nerves.

Even if you find it difficult to imagine yourself passing your exams, do you see how this kind of visualization can help you?

What you think about yourself is called your self-image because it's a picture you have of yourself in your mind.

Because your self-image is made up of thoughts, you also have the power to change it by creating new, different pictures of yourself, more in keeping with the way you want to be.

My guess is that you'll need some outside help to change your current self-image and that's one of the reasons I made the Audio Patch for you.

Use the Exam Magic Audio Patch to help yourself focus

The Exam Magic Audio Patch is a brilliant resource to help you manage your Fear Monkey. Listening to the Audio Patch helps you calm down and focus.

The Audio Patch is designed to help you not only calm down but also change your self-image so that you can reduce your fear enough to be able to do the work that will get you good results. The Audio Patch works whether you're used to getting high marks in the past and are afraid they'll slip, or you are used to getting low marks and are afraid the same thing will happen again.

Maybe you've had mixed results throughout your school years, and the low scores from the past are all you can think about. Whatever your situation, the Audio Patch is excellent at getting your mind to focus on a picture of you passing your exams with good grades. It works if you use it, so download it for FREE from **Google Play** or the **App Store** and start feeling better straight away.

Here's what students said about this problem:
'Reward yourself for good concentration.'

Exam Magic says:
Doing the work first and then rewarding yourself is a good habit to develop. You might also find it helpful to analyse why you're having trouble concentrating, so you can find the most useful ways to help yourself improve.

Assess the problem (and remember why you're doing all this work)
Do you mean that you can't concentrate at all, or that you can concentrate for only a short time? Can you concentrate on the subjects that interest you, but find that you drift off during classes on other subjects? (See

Problem #8, 'I find lessons boring.') Or does your attention wander no matter what you're doing?

Some things are easier to focus on than others. We can become so focused on a movie that we lose all sense of time. The same with video games and books and television and the Internet and so on. Concentrating on studying for exams takes work, though, so it requires a different approach.

It helps to be upfront about the distractions we all face. We've spoken about social networks and phones and worrying about failing. We've also discussed wanting a social life and spending time with boyfriends and girlfriends. We've covered TV, Saturday jobs, chores, sports and clubs, having better things to do, noise at home, not liking teachers, boring subjects, nagging parents... along with other things. Is it computer games, checking your emails, drinking tea, eating biscuits? Well, you know what's distracting you.

There are so many distractions that can take our attention away from the things we know we need to do. (See the chapters on Problems #16, #17, and #18 for more discussions on dealing with distractions.) That's why exam prep is an opportunity for you to learn some skills and attitudes that you'll be able to use long after you have finished full-time compulsory education. If you start with short periods and keep practicing, over time you can increase your capacity to focus and to concentrate on difficult things.

If you're struggling with focusing, you may even believe that you can't get better at it. A big tip here is to be very aware of whenever you tell yourself you can't get better at anything, because science tells us that you're mistaken. As I've mentioned, research tells us that the human brain has a huge capacity to learn new skills.

Improving on things we find difficult can feel like it's impossible, because learning and growing take effort and focus and determination. Yes, it can be hard work; it can make your brain and your body ache to force yourself to do the work to improve your academic skills and level of understanding—but it's not impossible.

There's a myth in society that some people are more talented or special than other people; some of these people we call celebrities. When we look at the lives of famous people, it might seem like fame and fortune fell into their laps without their having to put in any effort, but I'm not so sure that's the way it really is.

Famous people in the media who seem to spend most of their time partying, spending cash and breaking up with their partners are not, in my personal view, great examples of success, but I recognise that some people do aspire to being rich and famous. The myth is that some of them are famous for nothing and that somehow it's easy to live like they do. The truth is that even if they've just focused on being well known for the sake of it, becoming famous took effort and concentration, and staying famous is even harder.

Every goal takes effort.

Chunk your work down and develop a system
You can train yourself to focus even when your attention is wandering all over the place. Here's how:

- Chunk the time you spend studying down into shorter periods where you do specific tasks. If you're really struggling, chunk it down so that the challenges are so small that you'll get started on them. For instance, you might spend five minutes drawing one diagram from a science book, and then rest for a few minutes and come back and label it, and then rest and so on. It's better than doing no work.
- Work for a fixed length of time. Reward yourself after each study period, and be disciplined about it.
- Have a code or a set of rules you abide by. I can't tell you what that is—it's different for everyone, and you need to work out your own way of doing things. It could be something like 'I work for half an hour or more every night and no less'. In reality, you'll need to do more than half an hour's work, but it's better to do something rather than nothing to get the ball rolling. Make your system simple so that you'll stick to it.

You need to prove to yourself that you can give yourself a command and follow through. Even if it's a small change you make, it's taking you in the right direction.

You won't change everything overnight, but you can make incremental gains, small changes that add up over time and help you feel better about yourself. You'll learn that you do have the ability to push through and grow your sense of self.

Here's what students said about this problem:
'Start early and keep it up to fit it all in.'

Exam Magic says:
As you read through this book, you'll notice a pattern. All of the problems require you to step up and face them. Some problems are more sensitive and need you to be kinder to yourself, and some ask you to be more responsible.

What do you think of when you look at the word 'responsible'? If you associate it with lack of freedom, think again. Responsibility involves power and choice. Being able to choose your response to the things happening around you brings you *more* freedom, not less.

You can think, say and do the things that will lead to more and better exam results, or you can hand control over to whoever happens to be the best at attracting your attention, distracting you and using up your time. When you look for excuses, you give away your power to someone or something else.

If you've still got plenty of time before your exams, keep working. If it feels like it's too late, keep working.

You're doing this to earn qualifications and you're doing this to prove to yourself that you can trust and believe in yourself.

There genuinely is a lot to do to get ready for your exams. Anyone who thinks there isn't clearly hasn't taken any tests recently. Plus there's all of the other stuff that makes up your life as well!

Depending on how consistently you are working now and how well you worked in the past, you might find yourself with too much to do and not enough time to do it in. Even someone who has been working constantly can feel overloaded, especially as exams get closer.

Assess how you use your time now
First thing to do is to evaluate how you use your time.

Let's use the method I mentioned in the chapter on Problem #14. On a scale of zero to ten, where zero is 'I'm completely wasting all of my time—every minute' and ten is 'I don't waste any of my time at all', what number would you give yourself?

Write your number here: _____

Think about your wasted-time number. How low or high is it? If you gave yourself a six out of ten, for example, that would mean you're using your time 60 percent effectively and wasting 40 percent of your time. A number of eight or higher is what you should be aiming for (using 80 percent of your time effectively), as being distracted for more than 20 percent of your time is not going to be conducive to getting the best out of your study time.

What do you waste time on? Make a list of all the things you spend time doing that are of no use at all for passing exams. It could be something like:

- Watching TV
- Playing video games
- Using my phone
- Staring into space

What's on your list? Write it in the space below

Now look at your list. Are these things genuinely a priority for you now? Is it true that you can't live without them for a few weeks or months?

Make a plan
What will you do to free up more time for the things that will count in making your exam results the best they can be? What can you do to make things better for

yourself? Think about some action steps you can take to reduce the amount of time you waste and increase your exam preparation.

Your action steps don't have to be big things. One step might be that you turn off your social networks for half an hour or put your phone out of sight. You know what will work for you.

What isn't working is making excuses that you only half-believe anyway.

Write your thoughts below. What steps can you take?

I can...

Did you come up with at least one action step to help you use your time more effectively? Now go do it and notice how it changes the way you feel.

You may have to return to this exercise several times, and that's okay. As long as you identify what you can do to move things forward and then go do those things, you'll get better results than if you allow yourself to become distracted.

Here's what students said about this problem:
'Just think, "not much longer".'

Exam Magic says:
Our minds can trick us into believing all kinds of things which aren't true. This tough phase feels like it will last forever, but it won't. Ask for help. Break big tasks into smaller ones. Keep going. It's worth doing the work because more than anything else, you need to prove to yourself that you can make a difference and be brave and make good choices for yourself.

Are you tired because you're working long hours? It is possible to overdo it. We all need downtime to rest and recover. Exams are important, but they're not more important than your health and well-being.

If you're having trouble sleeping, here are a couple things to consider:

- Many of us have our laptops, tablets and phones with us nearly all the time. I've known students who stay up until the early hours of the morning keeping up to date with friends. Put your devices away thirty minutes or more before you get into bed to sleep, or at least use them to listen to some calming music. It's best not to watch moving images before sleep because they overstimulate your brain.
- You might find the Audio Patch useful. A lot of students use it to fall asleep to. It even works better while you're sleeping because it's designed to work with the part of your mind that never sleeps, your subconscious.

Or is your tiredness less physical and more emotional and psychological? For example, imagine that your alarm has just gone off for another school-day morning. You roll over to hit the snooze button. How familiar is that sleepy feeling? But what if your mum came in and told you she'd just won a fortune in the lottery? I bet the tiredness would vanish pretty quickly, don't you?

You've been in full-time education for a long time. If you are facing exams, then you're getting close to a lifetime milepost. It's okay to be tired, whether it's the physical type or emotional and psychological or all of it rolled up together. It could be a mix of everything, but you're so close to reaching that milepost that you've just got to keep going. You'll get to goof off in the summer. Yes, you're tired, but can you find the energy to keep moving?

115

Take things one step at a time, and do what you can to get some decent sleep.

Here's what students said about this problem:
'Love yourself.'

Exam Magic says:
If you were to do the best thing for yourself, what would that be?

I can't say for sure what the students meant when they gave the advice to love ourselves, but maybe it means to do the right thing for ourselves.

Remember that the right thing isn't always the easiest thing; it takes courage to face up to our responsibilities. Being more aware of the Fear Monkey's tricks can help us see things more clearly.

If you are struggling right now, you need support. Don't assume that people can look at you and know what you need without your asking for it. Most people, when under pressure, still care about others, but might not notice what's going on around them. Asking for support for yourself or another is a loving thing to do.

Remember what causes stress

Nearly everything we've covered in this book relates to stress in one form or another, but what do we really mean when we say we're stressed?

Have you ever finished your day feeling like the Fear Monkey has flung you around like a ragdoll or used you as its personal punching bag? It can get so you just want to sleep until it's all over, but with your mind racing like a mouse on a squeaky wheel, there's no rest in sight.

How am I doing? Is this anywhere near your experience?

We all know how it feels to be stressed, we each have our own versions of it, but what causes it? If you read the beginning sections of this book, you'll remember that stress is caused by our thoughts.

If the thought is a Fear Monkey thought that basically says, 'I'm in danger', our bodies release chemicals into our blood that, amongst other things, make our hearts beat faster. That feeling that we want to run away, hide or lash out is our much-talked-about flight-or-fight reflex.

We really ought to call it the 'fight, flight or hide' reflex.

The *hide* part is where we try to stay very still and our breathing becomes very shallow. You'll see mammals do it when they are being hunted by a predator. The problem with 'fight, flight or hide' is that it stands some chance of working if we're dealing with a hungry lion, but it's useless if the predator is our own thinking!

A bit of stress is okay, so that we know we're alive and there's a challenge ahead. Too much stress, and we can't think straight and we just want it all to go away.

Sometimes the things we do can, unfortunately, make the stress worse. TV shows, social networks, many websites, and the games and apps on our smartphones are made by businesses that can thrive financially only if they capture our attention. You already know that they are very good at getting our attention. They can also add to our levels of stress, either because of their content or because, as exams get closer, you find yourself watching TV or zoning out online instead of studying, and that heavy feeling starts to come down on you.

To reduce stress, we need to deal with its causes, which are our Fear Monkey thoughts.

Try out some of this book's suggestions
The Audio Patch is designed to help you cope with stress by giving your brain some calming input; it's made to help you pass your exams with the best possible grades. I know I keep going on about it, but it really does work!

It's clear that when we feel safe and peaceful, we are able to focus better. Calm, positive focus is the optimum state of mind in which to prepare for exams. It's the best state of mind to take exams in, too. Repeated listenings to the Audio Patch will help you achieve this state of mind.

Even if you put only one or two pieces of information from this book into practice, those small adjustments can make a big difference in your exam results. Everyone is different, so choose whatever feels true to you and act upon it. You'll feel better than if you allow your Fear Monkey to run wild.

You'll be okay. Whatever you do, just hang in there. If you're really worried about stress, show this section to an adult you trust and start a conversation about it. Sometimes all we really need is to feel that we're not alone with a problem and to know that someone else understands and cares about us.

There's a myth which people buy into about lone achievers who become successful all by themselves, without any help from anyone else. But if you look closely at the personal stories of anyone who's achieved something worth talking about, you'll always discover that they had people around who helped, supported and guided them.

In other words, nobody makes it entirely on their own. I wrote this book as my way of helping you through your exams so you wouldn't feel alone with them. Your school is also there to support you; can you find a way to ask for the help you need?

Here's what students said about this problem:
'Think, "What's the worst thing that could happen if I fail?"'

Exam Magic says:
This advice is well intentioned, but if you're worrying about the worst thing that could happen, you're probably already scaring yourself with mental movies based on the idea that your exams are the most important thing that will ever happen to you.

They're not.

You'll be okay no matter what happens in your exams.

They are important, but not more important than your health and well-being. This book was written to help you pass your exams, so let's be honest with each other. It feels horrible when exams go wrong, but the feeling passes eventually with time. Then when you feel better, you can look around and decide what to do next.

You learn from the experience and you move on. People respect this kind of strength, and frankly, if they don't, then that says more about them than it does about you! Leave them to deal with their own Fear Monkeys.

Students tell me that they sometimes feel pressured to pretend in front of their friends that they are not studying or that they don't care about exams. Maybe they want to act cool and keep up their reputation, because they think they'll be judged for working hard and putting social time second.

I'm reminded of Hannah's story. She was in the original group of students who asked me for help with their exams. Her situation was that she had got low grades in her mock exams. When I asked her about it, she said she didn't want to be judged or left out of social time with her group of friends. She feared that if she put studying above friendship, she'd be called names and left out.

She attended some Exam Magic lessons and I made the Audio Patch for her. Three weeks later, I asked her how things were going. She told me that instead of coming home from school and going on her phone or computer with her friends, she found herself getting out her books and getting down to her studies. She started to share what she was learning with Exam Magic, and her friends got interested, too. She even gave them the Audio Patch and they started using it. Pretty soon they were all studying and all of them got great grades.

Hannah changed her story by changing her thinking, and that spread to her friendship groups.

Understand how projection works

In reality, the stories we make up about what other people think about us are based on what we think about ourselves, not on what others are thinking. Psychologists call this kind of experience *projection*. It's as if we are the movie projector and we project what is in our minds out onto other people. For example, if we're feeling emotionally raw or fragile and a group are talking about a TV programme they saw last night and they laugh just as we happen to walk by, we might think they are laughing about or at us.

Has that ever happened to you?

Unless we actually ask someone what they're thinking, we're making it up. We can know someone so well that we get it right sometimes, but not all of the time.

Peer pressure is a very real thing for you because being accepted as part of a group feels really important, especially so when you are a teenager. Studying is mostly done on your own, and this is actually a big life lesson for you. There are times when we all need to do the right thing for ourselves, even if the people around us might not approve. One thing to keep in mind is that everyone you know at school is going through the same thing.

'I'm afraid of disappointing my parents'
Many students I've worked with have been afraid of letting their parents down. Their parents have high expectations for their exam results, and it's frightening to imagine not meeting those expectations. You might find that Problems #2, 'My parents nag me and don't understand the pressure I'm under', and #6, 'My parents compare me to my brothers and sisters', also relate to this issue.

Whether you're afraid of disappointing your parents or you're worried about someone else's opinion of you, the key thing here is to stop for a moment and think things through.

People are priceless and that includes you!
While it's absolutely true that all of us fall into the trap of judging ourselves negatively from time to time, it's also true that we're making a mistake when we do it.

If the brain in your head were a computer, it would be the most powerful and sophisticated one on the planet, and that's just your brain. Billions have been spent on trying to develop robots that can move and learn and communicate like humans. Although this technology is improving rapidly, it's nowhere near the sophistication we embody just by being alive.

Don't let the pressure about exams make you lose perspective on what really matters in life, and don't let your grades dictate your self-worth.

Don't mistake a school's judgments for your worth as a person

There is something that schools do that isn't very fair or nice, and that's to arrange students in lists with those with the highest marks at the top and those with the lowest marks at the bottom. Some subjects also put students in groups that everyone knows are top, middle and bottom, no matter what the school calls them. Our school uses colours, and if you are in anything called purple, you know you are at the bottom of the heap. How do you think it feels to be in the purple set for everything?

Schools have top groups and bottom groups and top of the class and bottom of the class and grades and scores, and so it's really easy to mistake these lists and your exam results for your worth as a person.

Some students get anxious because they've had good results in the past and are afraid that they'll slip down the rankings. There's also the opposite case. If you've decided that you're an outsider and that school is a waste of time and good grades are for geeks, will you allow yourself to do well in school? Do you worry that if you start to change your attitude and ask for help and start working, your friends will think you've sold out?

You can complete the following sentences to get a clearer picture of what you think your exam results will say about you.

If I get bad grades, people will think I'm ....

If I get good grades, people will think I'm....

Whatever you wrote is not what other people will think about you. It's what *you* think about you.

You can't control what other people think

We can't control what other people think of us, and as much as we might want to be liked and accepted, there's probably always going to be at least one person we don't see eye to eye with at one time or another. Do you know anyone whom everyone likes all of the time?

We each must learn to accept ourselves and care more about what we think of ourselves than about what anyone else does. It's our thoughts that we experience as feelings, and when we know this, it makes us more powerful. We can be aware of our thoughts and we can choose them. *Or, if we can't choose all of them—and I don't think we can control all the thoughts that pop into our heads— we can choose which ones to pay the most attention to, and decide which ones might be true and which ones are Fear Monkey lies.* How pleasant our thoughts are is reflected in how good we feel.

I don't want to pretend that it's easy to think this way and accept yourself as you are. I do want to appeal to your sense of fairness and reason. Is it a better idea to learn to accept that you are valuable just as you are, because you are alive and a human being with rights and dignity, than to judge yourself against exam results?

Sometimes it can be so difficult to be kind to ourselves. But will you stop being loved and cared for if your exam results aren't what you want? Will you be less of a human being than students with better marks?

Maybe it feels true, but is it?

Here's what students said about this problem:
'Stop pretending things will sort themselves out without your doing something about it.'

Exam Magic says:
This might sound odd from something called Exam Magic, but magical thinking—pretending that everything will be all right without any effort on your part—isn't going to get you through your exams. You have absolutely got to take action to change your results.

The real magic starts to happen when you take more responsibility for the way you think and act. Pretending something doesn't matter won't make it true. It does matter that you learn how to change things for yourself.

Even if it is too late to sort *everything* out, you can at least make a start.

Remember that the Fear Monkey deals in all-or-nothing thinking. Your Fear Monkey tries to get you to give up because it believes that's how to keep you safe. In reality, you can solve your problems one step at a time. Time is passing, exams are getting closer, and you can do something about it. There isn't a shortage of exam-prep materials anymore because you can look online.

The sooner you get help, the better.

What does it mean to feel unmotivated?

Originally I thought 'I have no motivation' and 'I can't be bothered' went together, but I think the use of language makes them different. Saying that you have no motivation—to my mind, anyway—acknowledges that you're aware there's a problem, but suggests that you feel disempowered to do anything about it. Saying you can't be bothered could mean exactly the same thing but also sounds like you don't care. I could be wrong, and it's probably also worth reading Problem #16 if you can be ... err ... bothered.

To take effective action on anything, we need three out of three of the following conditions:

1. We know what to do
2. We know how to do it
3. We know why we're doing it

When it comes to studying, how many of those three do you have? Is it just that you don't want to do it, or do you also need some help with knowing what and how to study?

Do you know why you're being asked to work for your exams? A lot of students think it's so that they can get good results and get a well-paid job, or that it's about going to university so that they can get a well-paid job. Maybe that's part of it, but it's not the whole picture. It's actually got a lot to do with learning to face challenges. Facing challenges is not easy. It's not meant to be easy. If it were easy, it wouldn't be a challenge and there wouldn't be much to learn from it.

You're being asked to put in a lot of effort to work at something and you've no guarantees it'll work out. Every challenge worth taking is like that.

I've spoken with young people who tell me they don't have any dreams or ambitions, but I just don't believe them. Inside everyone is something trying to shine out into the world. Sometimes it's the thing we've forgotten about or won't dare admit to because if we did, someone might try to crush it or, even worse, we'd have to give it up because it didn't work out.

Everyone has the experience of trying and failing at something. Failing can feel bad enough that we might decide to give up and not take any more risks and play it safe.

Sometimes people try to avoid failing by never trying in the first place. You can see the problem with this approach! Never trying or giving up guarantees that we stay stuck.

Did I get that right? Are you scared of failure or trying to avoid failure by doing nothing?

Giving up might feel like the safe option, but it's not. It feels like the safe option until we run out of excuses and ways to hide our unhappiness.

Giving up on this challenge now means that you'll have to come back later and learn the lessons the challenge has to teach you. You might as well face it now, the best you can. You'll do it imperfectly, because that's the way challenges are met.

You might feel stressed and scared with every step, but you can do it. Exam Magic is a system that's designed to help you. It was made to help my students because they couldn't get motivated, either. They were too afraid to believe in themselves. Exam Magic worked for them and it can work for you.

I'm sure you've asked yourself why you're doing this, but ask again.

'Why' is such a big motivator. If I have a strong enough why, I'll work out how and what as I go along. It's the 'why' that makes a person unstoppable.

So why prepare for exams?

Do it because you'll grow as a person. Do it so you'll learn about your own limits and how to go past them. Do it so you'll discover that you're braver and more intelligent than you knew. Do it because this is one of the few times in your life that you'll be given a whole team of people to back you and support you and it won't cost you a penny. Do it to prove to yourself that you can change things when you decide to.

You can find a reason to do this that's more than because you're being forced to do it, and more than because the adults at home and at school want you to.

Do it for you.

Here's what students said about this problem:
'Distract yourself by studying.'

Exam Magic says:
Distracting yourself by working hard is easier said than done, but it is possible. If you can chunk your studying down into manageable pieces, it ought to be possible to focus for short bursts of time. Sometimes it can be a relief to have something else to focus on, at least for a while.

When you've got a lot on your mind, what you're experiencing is a lot of thoughts whizzing around. Sometimes they get stuck; often they repeat over and over. When your mind is spinning, have you ever noticed that the thoughts are nearly always about the past or the future? Maybe you regret something you said when you were tired or angry or afraid, and you keep replaying the scene in your mind, wishing you'd said something different, or maybe you're worried about exams.

Remember that thoughts cause feelings. If you have a lot of pleasant thoughts running around in your mind, that feels great. 'I'm so happy my friends are doing well and my family is in great shape. I really feel good about my look and I'm looking forward to my holidays. I think the future is going to be amazing.' If you have a lot of unpleasant worry- or regret-filled thoughts running around in your mind, that feels bad. 'I'm not happy with my look, and I have too much to do, and the holidays are too far off, and there's never an end to the work.'

When we feel down, it's because of down thinking, and it can turn into a vicious cycle. We think about feeling down and that's a down thought and that takes us down further and it gets heavier and heavier, and before we know it, we've got too much on our minds and we can't remember what it felt like to feel okay.

This is not to make light of anyone's problems, because I don't know what they are. Without knowing the ins and outs of your personal situation, what I can say with confidence is that we all need a break from believing our negative thinking.

Have you ever been really worried about something, when something else takes your attention off it and you totally forget what you were worried about, at least for a moment? Maybe it comes back again, but that time without the worry is a chance for your body to recover and restore some of its strength.

One way to manage your mind is to keep a worry journal. Some cultures have worry dolls. They are tiny little figurines that you tell your worries to before you go to sleep at night. The dolls are then supposed to help you solve the problems while you get a good night's sleep. You can do a similar thing by keeping a worry journal. Many of my adult coaching clients find it very useful to write their worries in a book. Once your worry thoughts are written down, close the book and leave the thoughts inside on the page, safe and sound, for the night.

Sometimes our minds keep repeating things so that we'll pay attention to them and not forget them. If you write them down in a worry journal, the mind feels satisfied that those things are being taken seriously and you can get some peace. You can think of keeping a worry journal as a way of reassuring your Fear Monkey that you notice it, so it doesn't have to scream and shout so loud to get your attention. (For more on using journals to manage your feelings, also see Problem #6: 'My parents compare me to my brothers and sisters.')

Try using a journal; it might work for you.

PROBLEM #30: MY HORMONES ARE OUT OF MY CONTROL

Here's what students said about this problem:
'You're a teenager; get a grip!'

Exam Magic says:
What does 'get a grip' mean to you? If it means 'take control,' this sounds like a better way of going about things than feeling powerless.

Everyone's hormones are out of control! We don't get to decide how much of them we have or how they work in our bodies.

Have you ever been in a hall of mirrors at a fun fair? All the mirrors are distorted, so you get a distorted image of yourself coming back at you. The mirrors magnify your size and shape or make you look tiny, or as if you have massive, long, floppy arms and so on. Hormones can work like a hall of mirrors. They affect moods and distort the way we perceive ourselves and how we see ourselves in relation to others.

The only thing that is in our control is our response to the emotional effects of our hormones.

As humans we can see things both logically and emotionally. Logic and emotion are very different from one another. Our hormones affect our emotions, so we might feel overwhelmed or think that people are being unfair to us. We might feel out of control and panicked and have all kinds of negative ideas, but if we stop and look at the situation logically, we'll often see things differently.

Emotionally, it feels like your hormones are controlling you, but is that true? If you look at it logically, do you see that you have choices in the ways you respond to your emotions?

You might need a duvet day or a bowl of ice cream. Maybe you'll need to let some frustration and anger out. Get out of the house. Go for a walk or a run. Whatever you do, make sure it isn't hurtful to you or another being.

I'm not saying it's easy to change how we respond to our feelings; I'm saying it's possible.

Our lives are affected by the quality of the choices we make. It's very tempting to want to give up on the responsibility for choosing and to give it to things like hormones, or luck, or blaming others. Wouldn't it be better, though, to take more responsibility for yourself and join in the conversation about what's best for you? This way you'll have more choices about how your life turns out.

To choose something, we need to believe it's possible. Now that you've read this book, I hope you see more possibilities in front of you.

WHAT NEXT?

Writing things down accesses a different part of your brain than when you read something. Talking about it accesses another part, and when you put your learning into action, you're using a different area of your brain again. Thinking, speaking and doing are three of the things this book is encouraging you to do differently so that you feel better and get better exam results. I encourage you now to take a moment and write down your thoughts in response to the questions below. If you have someone to share your ideas with, I also urge you to discuss your answers with them.

1. What does "thinking about school in a different way" mean to you?
2. What advice would you give to someone who is struggling with their Fear Monkey?
3. What is schoolwork for and why are you doing it?
4. What's the best advice you could give someone who is getting ready to take exams?
5. If you were to change just one thing about the way you approach school now, what would you change and why?

Will you choose to experiment with some of the ideas in this book? Exam Magic is made exclusively of ideas which have been found to be true. I invite you to choose one or more of these ideas and test them for yourself.

To find out how to get more from Exam Magic, visit **www.exammagic.co.uk**.

Download the Audio Patch App from **Google Play** or the **App Store**.

CONSULTANCY

We are looking for schools and organisations that are 100 percent committed to the well-being and achievement of all their students in an inclusive way, and that appreciate the power of Exam Magic and peer mentoring.

Call 0208 720 7126 or email mike@exammagic.co.uk

SHARE THIS BOOK WITH OTHERS

Schools and organisations can purchase learning packs. Each pack includes downloadable copies and teaching resources.

Bulk purchases of this book are also available at discounted rates. For information on learning packs and bulk orders, email: sales@florencemaypublishing.com

FLORENCE MAY
Publishing

London

ABOUT THE AUTHOR

Michael Warwick is a teacher, life coach and therapist. Founder of Exam Magic and the Florence May Educational Consultancy, he works with schools and organisations that are 100 percent committed to the well-being and achievement of all their students in an inclusive way. Michael is a career psychologist at the City Of London Therapy Centre and in private practice at www.findyourselftherapy.com.

He lives in London with his partner, and when not working, loves walking with his dog and writing and performing music.

Connect with Michael

www.linkedin.com/in/michaelawarwick

mike@exammagic.co.uk

www.exammagic.co.uk

Lightning Source UK Ltd.
Milton Keynes UK
UKHW020919090919
349451UK00013B/542/P